# BEAT THE BOOKIES

## THE DO's AND DON'Ts OF SPORTS BETTING

# JOHN DUGGAN

POOLBEG

Published 2011
by Poolbeg Books Ltd.
123 Grange Hill, Baldoyle,
Dublin 13, Ireland
Email: poolbeg@poolbeg.com

A catalogue record for this book is available from the British Library.

ISBN 978-1-84223-446-4

Typeset by Patricia Hope in Sabon

Printed by
CPI Cox & Wyman, UK

**www.poolbeg.com**

## About the author

John Duggan has been Sports Editor of Ireland's national independent radio station, TODAY FM, since 2005. A graduate of Politics and Business from Trinity College Dublin, he has worked as a broadcast journalist and sports reporter for twelve years. He is the Executive Producer of *Premier League Live* on TODAY FM and is a regular contributor to the *Ian Dempsey Breakfast Show* and the *Ray D'Arcy Show*. He was born and lives in Dublin.

# Acknowledgements

There are many people I would like to thank for helping me write this book. So if I have forgotten you I apologise in advance. Specifically I would like to thank Ian Dempsey for making it happen, Mario Rosenstock, Martin Maguire and Paul Collins on the TODAY FM *Breakfast Show*. Also at TODAY FM, I would like to thank Willie O'Reilly and Caroline Davies for their support. I would like to express my sincere thanks to Poolbeg Publishers, specifically Kieran Devlin, Paula Campbell, Gaye Shortland and David Prendergast for their help along the way.

Gratitude must also go to the following who were of great assistance during the project: Johnny Lyons, Simon Lougheed, Stephen O'Connor, Sohan Basu, Jonathan Mullin, Ricky Delaney, Paddy Power, Ken Robertson, Barry Orr, Dee 'Lemonade' Costello, Anne-Marie, Caroline and Helen, and last but not least Róisín Ní Mhórdha, who was a constant source of support and inspiration as I tore my hair out.

*For my mother*

# CONTENTS

# Prologue

## Flesch for Fantasy

*Flesh, Flesh for Fantasy*
*We Want*
*Flesh, Flesh for Fantasy*
*We Want*
*Flesh, Flesh for Fantasy*
*You Cry*
*Flesh, Flesh for Fantasy*

Billy Idol, 1983

### A Free Golfing Lesson

My father passed away in November 2002. We had a relationship that would be best described as an old-school Irish Catholic bond between father and son, in that emotions are rarely shown, and other things bring you close together. In our case it was a shared love of hurling, horse-racing and gambling. My first memory of a race was the 1986 Aintree Grand National, when West Tip won for jockey Richard Dunwoody, and the

1

race that got me hooked on having a flutter was the 1997 Grand National, when Lord Gyllene won by half the track at 14/1. As a first-year college student, I pocketed fifty punts for my troubles, which was enough then to keep me in alcohol for a week.

A few years later, the euro and the Celtic Tiger had arrived and £50 was not enough. I wanted more bang for my buck and in 2003 there was a bit of money sloshing around the estate. With my head not exactly in the right place and having more money than sense, I was punting quite heavily at the time, mainly on horses and golf. I backed the winner of the Scottish Grand National in April, a horse called Ryalux at 7/1, and made a four-figure sum. That was also the first proper tip I gave on the radio.

At the beginning of May in that year, there was a golf event on the US PGA Tour, called the New Orleans Classic. It was a run-of-the-mill tour stop, with none of the big names like Tiger Woods in the field. However, I did have my eye on a guy by the name of Steve Flesch, who had never won on the US Tour. He was *the* quintessential journeyman, finishing in the Top 10 a staggering 38 times in tournaments without winning. He had posted two Top-10 finishes in April, and his record at the course, English Turn, was very good. He finished second there in the event in 1998 and 1999, and sixth in 2000. Available at odds of 50/1, he jumped off the page at me.

I was convinced. I remember telling a couple of people at the time to get their money on Steve Flesch. I would call it a gambler's premonition. Sometimes you just have a feeling. So I went and put €500 on the nose on Flesch to win at 50/1.

On the final day of the tournament, Flesch was seven shots off the lead and my money looked to be toast. When I came home from work at around 10 p.m. he was 7 under par for his round and just a shot behind the leader, Scott Verplank. I sat motionless, churning inside, and watched as Flesch saved par on 18 to finish on 21 under par. Verplank was 22 under par with three holes to play before making bogey, double bogey. So it transpired that Flesch was in a sudden-death play-off with another American, Bob Estes.

"Why didn't I go each way?" I thought to myself as both players found the fairway and then the green. Flesch was further away from the hole, about 35 feet, so he was to putt first. It was a great stroke, and as the ball glided towards the cup I knew it was in. I jumped up from my bed and started screaming "Get in the f****** hole!" as the ball disappeared. I kept on repeating that mantra until my mother came up the stairs, wondering what all the commotion was. I screamed "Get in the f****** hole!" at her before going back to watch Estes miss his putt. I knew he would miss. Flesch had won and the next day I collected a cheque for €25,500 from Paddy Power Bookmakers. It was a frightful amount of money and a surreal 24 hours. I didn't get much sleep. The high was incredible, like nothing I have experienced before or since. Pure adrenalin.

I recounted the story to a cousin (who is a shrewd punter) a couple of years later and he told me that I was an idiot. He was absolutely right. The moral of the story is that what I did was a little insane. I might as well have gone into a newsagent and purchased a lotto ticket. It was gambling on whimsy, placing a disproportionate stake on a tournament containing 150 players and not spreading the risk by going each way. It was a bit of a fluke. Yes, I had done my research and had a good feeling, but it's the type of gambling that catches up with you very quickly. Don't get me wrong, I didn't blow the winnings. But in hindsight, I was very lucky. In 2003, when I started tipping on the airwaves, I couldn't have given sage advice to anyone about betting. I was both fearless and undisciplined. Fearlessness is to be admired and it can get you some of the way down the road. However, in the end, indiscipline will beat it every time.

I've learned down through the years by observing my behaviour and that of others. I see guys in betting shops rushing up to the counter with a scribbled docket to have money on before the greyhound bell goes. I've watched them all afternoon backing horses left, right and centre. They even back the virtual racing. It's not good gambling. It's not fun. It's from the Steve Flesch School of Punting.

For eight years I've been giving a weekly tip on the *Ian Dempsey Breakfast Show*, on Ireland's National Independent Radio Station, TODAY FM, where I'm the

Sports Editor. The 'Tip of the Week' is designed to be a bit of fun, so that listeners with an interest in a sporting event can make a few bob by my pointing them in the right direction. It's not to be taken too seriously, so I don't tip odds-on shots (bets at less than even money) or highlight what I would call 'Mickey Mouse' events, like the 4.23 dog race at Romford or a pre-season soccer friendly.

I reported on the Cheltenham Horse Racing Festival in 2002 and 2003 and gave some winners. Ian then asked me to give a weekly bet, and in 2003 and 2004 I made a profit. In 2005 and 2006 I began to lose my confidence and the winners dried up. I was given a hard time by the listeners who texted into the show. I was getting flogged every week. From time to time I am given a monkey (i.e. €500) a day by Paddy Power Bookmakers to bet with for charity. Luckily I got out of jail at Christmas in 2006 by tipping a horse called The Listener to win the Lexus Chase at Leopardstown at 8/1. The €4,500 collected for charity from the €500 outlay was enough to keep me in a job.

However, to keep my bets in check, I needed a marker, a mythical amount on which to base my selections and focus the mind. The talent was there but not the structure. In 2007 I started with a 'virtual money' bank of €500 and notionally broke even that year. In 2008 I made a profit of €1,020 from a starting 'virtual money' bank of €1,000, a return of over 100%. In 2009 I made another €500 profit from a bank of €1,000, a return of 50%. In 2010, I was making a loss with three months to go, which I will come to later. One can fall out of form, and that's when you rein in and significantly lessen the money you wager.

My sister has been a bank manager for over twenty years. She tells me – as I am sure you all know – that the greater the risk, the greater the reward. Betting is risky, because there is no guarantee of success, unlike a low-yielding deposit account. Even with a poorly performing share investment, it's unlikely that you would lose much, but you may not gain much either. With betting, you can lose everything, so it's important to strictly monitor your conduct. The battle is to beat that stingy rate of deposit interest.

I have never included occasional charity bets in my 'virtual money' profit and loss figures. I am given €2,000 by Paddy Power to bet with for charity every year for four days at Cheltenham and €1,000 every year for two days at Galway. If I lose the money, I lose the money. If I win, the returns go to a nominated charity. It's more pressure than usual as charities are involved and I could actually make a difference to somebody's life, rather than my own. I have noticed that when I am under the gun, I tend to deliver more. For seven years of the last nine I have made a profit for charity on the Cheltenham Festival and I have also turned a profit from four of the last five years at the Galway Races. So my experiences got me thinking that by imparting all the principles I have learned down through the years about sport and betting, I could explain the opportunities and pitfalls of this very popular Irish pastime.

A lot happens every sporting year, so the objective of this book is to examine not just betting itself, but how to gain an edge on the events which reoccur and generate the most interest. I will specifically examine National Hunt and Flat Racing, Soccer, US PGA Tour Golf, the GAA Championships, Rugby, Tennis and the Four Golfing Majors. I'm sorry, but Athletics, Snooker, Boxing, Formula One, Greyhounds and Darts didn't make the cut. You have to factor a degree of specialisation into what you do.

This book is not intended to be time-specific, as the identification of champions and the regaling of sporting stories has been going on for years, but we'll look at 2010, as the most recent data provides us with the best clues for beating those mean bookies and reducing their profit margins! I am constantly learning about sports betting – the good choices I have made – the mistakes. I want to pass on my experiences, significant or not, to help you in your decision-making. Good luck!

# Part 1

*The Tools*

# Chapter 1

## The Mind

Ireland is a sports-mad nation. The evidence is empirical. Sport is magnificent. It brings people together, participants and supporters. Sport allows people to belong, at a young age or in adult life, by being a fan of a county team, or a national side, or an international star. A sports fan lives for the occasion, the result and the social currency which each event brings. Look what boxing did for race relations in the United States in the 1960s – or what rugby did for South Africa in 1995. Irish people may have listened to the commentary of Ronnie Delany's Olympic 1500 metre win in Melbourne in 1956, watched Ray Houghton score against England at Euro '88, cheered home Sonia O'Sullivan in Sydney in 2000, or willed Padraig Harrington to win his first major golf championship in 2007. All memorable days.

Sport thrives on its unpredictability – even the actors themselves don't know what is going to happen on the day. I remember the 2001 UEFA Cup Final. Liverpool were playing Alaves. I was tired after a morning shift. I wasn't in the humour to watch it. So I took forty winks. When I woke up, to my amazement, Liverpool were lifting the trophy after a 5-4 win.

We Irish also have a love for betting. There is a roguish element to the Irish psyche. We relish fun and the idea of a flutter, on the horses or on the Lotto. Irish Bookmakers turn over an estimated €4.5 billion each year, so don't tell me that the betting industry in this country isn't big business. When you combine a sporting event, which is subject to chance, with betting on sport, which is about trying to predict the outcome of an event, it's an intriguing combination.

The majority of sports fans are male. And almost all sporting gamblers are male. I am not speaking for every man out there, but as a regular gambler I know a lot about betting. In my opinion it is the battle, Man v. Bookie, which is attractive for many punters. Vanity plays a part as using your judgement to play God and watch the outcome you foresaw materialise is empowering. Then there is the matter of money. The possibility of changing one's fate by risk alone can be intoxicating, which is why some people gamble again and again. However, this book is not geared towards those of you who gamble for the thrill, for those who are addicted to risk. I'm always ruminating over the seduction of betting to the masses. It has its supporters; it has its detractors. The Islamic world does not approve of gambling and it's frowned upon by Buddhists and Mormons. Internet betting is banned in the United States. My own view is that life in essence is about our reaction to the idea of control, because what is already decided for us is our death. Therefore, while we are living, I think we naturally strive for personal control. To choose who to relate to emotionally and mentally, where to reside, what to eat, what to drink, what career to choose. Of course, a lot of choices are made for us by circumstance and nurture. And in a world where we have to conform to the rule of law, to the rules of society, independence and self-expression play a vital role in our individuality and sanity. The choice to involve risk in our lives can be a very liberating experience.

I've never been a compulsive gambler. As with alcohol, if you bet in moderation, it can be very enjoyable. Those of us who enjoy a tipple may go overboard from time to time, and it's natural for any callow gambler to open the compulsive door, take a look around, and then hopefully shut it again without too much of a hole in his pocket. Genetically, there will always be addicts. My view is that betting is dangerous for those who develop a problem with it because, if it becomes an addiction, it's the only addiction where you believe you can cure yourself by indulging even more in the activity. So a problem gambler carries a strain of self-destruction. It's all about the 'big win' that will make everything okay, mentally and financially. The 'big win' will bring vindication for the addict. He or she (and it's almost always a he) may feel that the next win is around the corner and, when it doesn't arise, the gloom deepens. All money earned is regenerated into the fund to go for the 'big win'. Of course, the idea of a 'big win' is folly because someone who is aiming for that is unlikely to be thinking clearly, placing their money rationally and selecting the right event. The problem is that addicts are out of control – that's why they are addicted.

For about a year after the Steve Flesch win, I engaged in bouts of what I would call 'binge gambling'. I know what it is like to 'lose it' at the races. To give you an example, in 2003, to date the first and only time I went to the Galway Races, I brought a lot of money and it was a hedonistic affair. I was sharing a room with my work colleague Paul Collins, and he described my behaviour akin to that of George Best as I stumbled in at all hours, worse for wear, with wads – and I mean *wads* of cash. "Where did it all go wrong?" he asked ironically. Paul then rang me on the Friday wondering where I was. "I'm going home," I said. Enough said. The money I had won earlier that week was gone and more besides. The day before, I wasn't in the best frame of mind and I began to lose a lot of money at the course. Once I started to lose, my mood darkened. I was on my own and I wasn't enjoying myself. I didn't want to speak to anyone – the exchange of a pleasantry would have been far too much to bear. I felt very alone in a crowd of thousands. I didn't want to have a drink and smile – all I wanted to do was gamble and try and win back what I had lost. As the rain soaked my suit, I thought, "How miserable do I feel right now?" So my answer was to leave the premises. As I left Galway, I reflected negatively on a wasted week.

When I look back, nearly eight years on, I shake my head and think "Was that me?" So now, I don't see that as a wasted week at all. I am glad I have had the experience of reckless gambling, because I tend to be naturally analytical and self-analysis can be cathartic. Years of experience and maturity have shaped me into a far better bettor. I find it very easy to maintain my discipline nowadays. I find it just as enjoyable giving a tip as placing a bet. Over the past six years I have developed and aimed to perfect a completely different outlook against the backdrop of a weekly tip in the public domain. I am not interested in waking up the next day after 'losing it' at the track or on the internet. I am not interested because it's a horrible, depressing feeling, thinking of the money that was there just hours ago. In racing parlance, it's called 'doing your brains' – when irresponsible decisions result in wasted money. From my (thankfully rare) experiences of losing money the wrong way in the past, I can remember how the money felt unclean in my mind and I wanted the day to end, so I could press the reset button on a new chapter with new money. When the money was gone, it was actually a relief, because there was no more that could be lost in a negative frame of mind as a result of sheer stupidity. Losing that way was an awakening.

There's no doubt in my mind that compulsive behaviours are the fast track to the poorhouse. I strongly believe that sports betting is a long-term game – so you must immediately, by default, set your expectations at a low level. I advocate a sensible, healthy approach to sports betting for those who are looking for a sustainable 'edge' on the bookmakers. There's a scene in the movie *Bad Lieutenant* where the protagonist – an officer of the law played brilliantly by Harvey Keitel – completely loses it. His 'double or quits' gambling on a fictional game between baseball teams the New York Mets and the LA Dodgers takes on devastating proportions. Keitel's character keeps losing and he owes the wrong people money. So placing his life in the hands of hitter Darryl Strawberry, he gets in way over his head. The iconic scene is when Keitel – high as a kite on illegal substances – listens to Strawberry mess up the game on his car radio. He shoots the radio in a fit of instant rage, turns on the siren after realising his actions, and begins howling like a child as he races through New York, cursing Strawberry for putting him in an impossible position, a situation which has dire consequences for him. That was a work of fiction, but the sad truth is that some gamblers love the risk. If the euphoria of winning to recover from the desolation of losing is what you crave, then you are probably on a carousel. I will give a lot of prosaic advice in this book, but the best advice I could give to any gambler on the edge is to get off the carousel. It's a waste of time.

Now a lot of sports fans may throw a fiver on a match or a horse for recreation. They may not expect to win but it increases their enjoyment of the event. And that's fine. However, the person who bets for recreation isn't likely to win in the long run. You often hear TV personalities using the expression "If I was a betting man . . ." and you know by default that they don't bet. I wouldn't classify the man who bets for recreation as a betting man. A betting man for me is someone interested in making money, burnishing their ego, or experiencing the thrill, or perhaps a combination of all three.

I will make my position crystal clear at this point. All I am interested in from a betting perspective is profit. It's the Number 1 policy on my betting manifesto. I don't want to win for the sake of winning alone. I want to win in the long run. The satisfaction I gain is from making money. And the satisfaction I ultimately gain is from spending that money on a nice holiday or material goods. That to me is the visceral pleasure. Of course the joust with the bookies is enjoyable, but it's not the focus. People may ask me at the races, "Did you back any winners?" I would rather ask them, "Did you turn a profit?" If I am not making money on personal bets, I leave the game for a while until I can spot an opportunity. I am constantly researching, so the opportunities do present themselves. And as far as I am concerned, the only consideration you should have when you bet is profit. Not winning, not losing: *profit*.

# Chapter 2

## *The Fundamentals*

I have never had any interest in being a professional gambler. I would find it terribly mundane sitting alone in a room, working very hard (you have to do that in any job), betting on poor racing, not knowing where the next win was coming from. I expect it would lead to boredom, anxiety and poor decision-making. I prefer to engage in my current work and succeed at that. However, I do enjoy the idea of supplementing my income to a small degree by winning money on sports betting.

Is it for you? Is gambling for you? It may not be, and that's just the way it is. Before we analyse sports in detail, we have to adhere to what I believe are the key components required to have any chance of making this game pay. I will try to help, but please don't let the bookies gain an advantage from the off by ignoring simple rules. We are dealing with money here, so it's important not to throw it away.

## *Discipline*

No, I am not talking about some type of fetish, or the quality required to go running in the woods at 4 a.m. The first thing you need to do is to take an imaginary branding-iron and stamp the word *Discipline* into your soul, leaving a permanent mark.

What is dangerous about sports betting is that it can be quite a lonely pursuit. Perhaps it's the male ego, but *I* is often our favourite letter in the betting alphabet. "*I* worked it out." "*I* was right." "*I* took the money from the bookmaker." A lot of gamblers observe a friend winning and congratulate him. I wonder how many are secretly thinking, "The lucky sod, I wish that was me." It amuses me when people ask my opinion on a race, and no sooner have I started to answer, they are giving their own. Males are competitive, so it's human nature for a gambler to plough his own furrow. Go into a betting shop and you will see everyone in their own world. At the races, the time just before a race starts can be quite solemn, as the crowd anticipates the denouement. For the most part, gambling is not a shared activity, which means that being disciplined is all down to you.

Having a bet is meant to be enjoyable (note the difference between enjoyment and recreation) and you should never bet more than you can afford. If you don't have discipline – if you don't know when to stop – or if you can't follow a plan – you can just forget it. I know from personal experience that a weekly bet on the radio where I am constantly putting my neck on the line breeds caution.

If you give yourself a chance by being prudent you can discover if you are any good or not. On the other hand, as a strong libertarian, I believe there is nothing worse than sanctimony and do-gooders who shake their heads and sigh and mutter "It's a mug's game" or "A fool and his money are easily parted". I mean, I don't stop every smoker on the street, grab the cigarette out of their hands and extinguish it in front of them because it is bad for their health. It's none of my business. Also, there is a fine line in society between admiration for those who win and disdain for those who lose.

There is money to be made in sports betting, if you have a combination of knowledge, the ability to learn, the courage of your convictions and discipline. And discipline is step one on the journey. This isn't roulette or poker. You are not required to wear shades at all times and call yourself 'Johnny the Greek' for the benefit of the television cameras. It's sport, which you may know a lot about already. And with betting, nothing is set in stone. There are no right answers or Royal Flushes. You are spending your hard-earned money. So forget about life-changing wins and get to work. There's a reason why I have lower-denomination notes than €500 displayed on the cover of this book. *Discipline.*

## Keeping Records

I like to talk to fellow punters about their methodology. If I respect a punter, I want to know what makes them tick. Never stop observing. I once met an interesting man on the plane home from Cheltenham. He was a successful businessman, and he showed me a little red book of recorded bets. He knew what he was doing, right and wrong, and I admonished myself for not doing likewise. Not long ago, I requested my records from the betting exchange Betfair going back to 2003. Examining my track record post-Flesch was quite startling. I was surprised to see how much money I had made on soccer betting, but some of the early losing decisions on the horses were embarrassing. Making a note of every bet is a key component of being disciplined. People love to talk about their wins, and that's great, but how many of them know their profit and loss for the year? How many people who bet on sport can tell you what they did this time one year ago? I now record my bets, and even so I made a big mistake in the summer of 2010 by not consulting my picks for the Travelers Golf Championship from 2009. I tipped Bubba Watson in 2009 (he came 14th) but I must have been looking for a 200/1 rag (complete outsider) in 2010, being too clever by half. It was a very costly mistake, as I would probably have had something on Watson had I checked my notes from the year before. Instead, I didn't back him and he won at 50/1.

At least I have records, so I know it will pay off in time. What if I had no records? It's not easy to remember who you may have backed to win the 2007 Ulster Senior Football Championship, but if you have notes, then you may glean a nugget of information to help you.

## *Staking*

Another part of being disciplined, which is intertwined with recording your bets, is to monitor your stakes – or, in plain English, the money you put down. I can speak with confidence about this, because after two fantastic years of tipping, I became a little cocky on the *Ian Dempsey Show* in 2010, expecting to rack up a big profit on golf betting early in the year. It didn't happen and, as a consequence, I was making a mythical loss from my bank of 'virtual money'. A big part of this was down to the amount I was recommending on these golfers each week. Instead of reducing my stakes from €20 each way to €10 each way when I was losing, I often increased them to €30 each way, in the expectation that I would come good. It didn't happen (on air at least). So the question I have asked myself and will generally ask is: What's the point in keeping your stake for each bet between January and April at €10 and then putting €500 on a 'certainty' in May which loses? Why would you put €20 on one outcome and €100 on another? Where's the rationale? It's important to build a staking plan from your bank, deciding how much should go on each sport – and sticking to it. I often invest a lot of money in golf tournaments because I believe I have a talent for it and it's my best chance of making a return. I believe it's easier to make money on the US PGA Tour than, say, the Galway Races, so a staking plan must be built for you to monitor your progress. In 2010, I was off kilter with my staking, to my cost. There has to be structure with staking, a system whereby you have a certain amount in your bank and you spend a percentage of that bank over time. So as far as I'm concerned, I believe in (and try to adhere to!) holding at least 50% of my bank at all times. It's important to remain in the game.

## No Emotion

Do you remember the science-fiction film *Blade Runner*? There were characters in the movie called 'replicants' who escaped from an 'off-world' colony to find their creator on earth and force him to expand their predetermined four-year life span. The 'replicants' looked like humans and displayed every other human attribute apart from emotion. In betting you have to become a 'replicant'.

One of the biggest mistakes a punter on sport can make is to become emotionally involved in the bet before it is placed. And that's not easy, because when you are shouting for a team, a horse or a golfer, it's human nature to become emotionally involved. If you like your sport, you would probably do so anyway, even if there was no money on. And it's fine to do it, once the cold analysis has been completed and you are satisfied that you've placed a respectable wager. Of course you can be ecstatic if you win, but it's important to keep the highs low and the lows high. It's vital not to become emotionally involved because you think you see a certainty and then, when it doesn't win, you begin to change your stakes. Money has to be respected. It's easy in an online situation to see 50.00 as just numbers, and

23

not a physical note or the equivalent of ten pints over the week, or a nice meal with your lady and a bottle of wine. If you have a losing bet, remember that you can walk away. It's much better to make €200 over twelve months by punting sensibly and enjoying your Christmas than making €2,000 rapidly and losing it hastily. If you go to the races, don't try and bet on every race, don't throw good money after bad and try not to bet while inebriated! You can quickly lose the run of yourself and be down a lot of cash. One week's money doesn't carry more weight than the next week's. Emotion is not your friend, which means that you cannot become upset if you are unlucky.

Another strong issue with emotion is that gambling should never affect one's mood. If you lose and find yourself snapping at your other half, or are walking around with a thunderous cloud over your head, then this ain't for you! A bad day is a bad day – and nothing more. Impatience to gamble at the expense of all other daily tasks and irritability because of gambling are warning signs. If you marry discipline with controlled emotion, you cannot possibly lose your shirt.

## Examining your Losses

I have already touched upon how one can lose the wrong way. What's wrong with losing the right way? Unless you have gone bankrupt or have lost more than you can afford, it's not a problem. Don't take the Alpha Male approach to betting. It's not a contest. Someone who is not upfront about their losses is insecure. Never lie, never exaggerate, and never deflect from the real story. Yes, I had a disastrous Cheltenham in 2010. So what? I had made profit in the previous seven years out of eight. A lack of confidence in your own ability, processing too much information, and being out of luck can contribute to losing, apart from the general pitfalls I have touched upon.

Another thing to remember: don't get greedy. Just because you get the breaks one month doesn't mean it will be like that for the next six months. Stick to your plan. The key thing is to maintain your composure when things are not going your way. When the gods are not on your side, it's easy to try too hard, but don't let bad breaks defeat you. Luck, like everything, evens itself out in betting. The harder you work, the luckier you will become.

## Patience

In the pursuit of my favourite word, *profit*, there is always another day. That should be the daily slogan on the wall for any prospective gambler. It's the greatest thing I have ever learned in betting. I love to hear about the person who goes to the races and doesn't have a bet. The person who waits, and waits, and waits, and then strikes. You need to have a snail's patience, because you don't have to bet. If you have 5 bets a year and 4 of them win, it can often pay more than the person who places 5,000 bets. The time for patience is when you feel something will happen and you are happy to wait forever for it to happen. Of course, the risk is that it

may never happen. But it will happen. You may ask ten
girls out and they all say no. And then the eleventh girl
says yes and you have backed a winner. I can point to
my own experience in sport: when I backed Phil
Mickelson at Augusta, Comply Or Die in the Grand
National, Roger Federer to win his first Wimbledon and
Ireland's rugby players in the Grand Slam Year, I had a
good feeling in advance about them all.

Patience is also related to another bane of the regular
bettor, a lack of confidence. I find it frustrating when I am
not tipping winners on the radio. As I mentioned before, I
couldn't tip to save my life for the most part in 2005 and
2006. During the writing of this book, I had hoped to
simultaneously tip some big-priced winners and ride a
wave, as had been the case for the previous two years. The
winners didn't come. They weren't as frequent because I
was trying too hard. Sometimes you can be just a little bit
out of sorts in using your judgement and it's the difference
between winning and losing. This is where discipline and
staking levels come in. When I feel that I cannot see where
the next winner will come from, I try to decrease my stakes
and relax. I know my subject matter, so it's a case of
waiting and just letting it happen until the confidence
returns and the winners become easier to spot.

## And finally...
## Knowledge

Forgive me for stating the obvious, but the more you
know about the sport you are betting on, the better you

will do. Knowledge of your subject matter is mandatory if you are going to part with your money. If you are a beginner, it's best to bet with pennies – or better still, matchsticks – as you make mistakes along the way and learn from them. If you are an expert on a certain sport, stick to that sport in the pursuit of profit. I don't bet on boxing matches or on greyhound racing or on the NFL for the simple reason that I don't know enough about each sport to risk losing money, especially when the bookmaker is guaranteed to be more informed than me. If you keep records, you will soon discover where your talents lie, and you may be surprised to learn that you could make more money from betting on soccer, even though you naturally believe you are more of a rugby expert.

# Chapter 3

## *The Methods*

### Types of Bets

The most popular bets with bookmakers are 'win' and 'each way' bets.

A **win bet** is simply that. So for example, Don't Push It won the 2010 Aintree Grand National at 10/1. If you placed €10 on Don't Push It, you would receive €110 (€100 plus your €10 stake).

A **place only bet** on a horse race is for the horse to finish in the first 3 or 4, depending on the number of runners; in golf, a place bet is usually for the golfer to finish in the first 5. Even if the horse or golfer wins, you still only collect the place part of the bet. A €10 place only bet on Don't Push It at a quarter of the odds (1/4) of 10/1 would give you €35 back (€25 plus your €10 stake).

An **each way bet** is two bets: a win bet and a place bet, so your stake is doubled. A €5 each way bet costs

€10, and so on. So if you placed €5 each way on Don't Push It rather than €10 to win only, you would receive €72.50. (This is calculated by adding the win part of the bet, €55, to the place part of the bet, €17.50.) If Don't Push It finished third, you would lose the €5 you placed on the win part, but you would win the place part of the bet.

As punters can get their money back and usually a little more with a successful each way bet, bookmakers hate 'each way'. At 4/1 or over, it's a great insurance bet if your selection doesn't win, but comes close, especially for big-priced outsiders. In 2007, I tipped Turpin Green each way for charity at 66/1 for the Cheltenham Gold Cup on the morning of the race. I really fancied the horse, despite the price, and my €100 each way stake returned €1,750 when he finished third.

A **win double** is where you select two outcomes to occur, i.e. €10 on Arsenal to beat Chelsea at 2/1 and then Manchester United to beat Liverpool at 6/4. If your first bet wins, the €30 return from the Arsenal bet goes on Manchester United at 6/4. If United win, your total return is €75. An easy way to calculate this is to add 1 to the numerator part of the fraction (the top part) and multiply it by the stake to give you a decimal return (i.e. €10 X 3.0 X 2.5 = €75). Both of your bets must win for you to collect the double.

It then gets a little more complicated, when we examine multiple bets, in the form of accumulators and combination bets. If you select 4 football teams to win in a coupon, that's a **four-fold accumulator**. If only 3 of them win, then you lose the bet, but if all 4 win, the odds can be decent.

In horse-racing, a lot of punters invest in **Lucky 15** bets, where they select 4 horses and combine 4 single bets, 6 doubles, 4 trebles and 1 four-fold accumulator. The amount of bets adds up to 15 for a win-only Lucky 15, so an each-way Lucky 15 totals 30 bets which can provide nice compensation if you don't manage to pick all 4 winners, or if you decide to select a few outsiders and go each way. So in a win-only Lucky 15, if you had €1 on a 2/1 shot, a 7/1 shot, a 10/1 shot and a 16/1 outsider, and if you have 2 winners (2/1 and 10/1), you would receive a return of €47. Try and work it out! It's good practice!

A **Yankee** (11 bets) is a Lucky 15 without the singles. If you select all 4 winners in a Lucky 15, you are usually in line for a significant payday. A **Patent, Canadian, Heinz, Super Heinz and Goliath** are explained in the Glossary at the end of the book, along with common slang for money in betting.

A lot of bookmakers believe multiples are 'mug' bets, as the probability of selecting 4 winners is a lot less than picking 1. And the bookmakers offer percentage bonuses in the rare event that you have a winner on every line of a multiple coupon. Some bookmakers even pay treble the odds if you have only 1 winner in a Lucky 15. Thus there is merit in the argument that these bets should be avoided. I mean, why do they try to entice you with these bonuses in the first place?

However, multiples can come off spectacularly. At Cheltenham in 2005, I did a £1 each way Lucky 63, selecting 6 horses that day and investing £126 of the Queen's finest. I picked 3 winners: Moscow Flyer to win the Champion Chase at 6/4, Trabolgan to win the Novices' Chase at 5/1, and Idole First to win a Handicap Hurdle at 33/1. That 33/1 winner increased my potential return significantly. My horse in the final leg, De Soto, went off at 20/1, and was narrowly beaten by an Irish horse called Missed That. Indeed. If De Soto had won, I would have collected £15,000. Instead, I pocketed £1,500, which wasn't bad, but bad enough for me to shout "You've just cost me fifteen grand!" at the trainer of Missed That, Willie Mullins, in the winners' enclosure. Let's just say he looked at me with a bemused expression on his face.

## The Transaction

### The Betting Shop

Where do we get it on? I'm always amazed at the amount of people who, faced with the conundrum of how to place a bet, haven't a rashers. Going into a betting shop for them is like visiting Saturn.

There are 4 principal ways to bet in the modern era. The first is in the betting shops, or the bookie's. The second is over the phone. The third is online. And the fourth is, for horse and greyhound racing specifically, at the track.

Here is the dummies' bit if you have never darkened the door of a betting shop before. You may have received a tip for a horse in the Grand National. All you need to do is pick up a blank slip, write down the time of the race, the track, the name of the horse, the price (in other words the odds), what type of bet it is (win or each way) and how much money you want to have on (the stake). Then confidently walk to the counter and you will be handed a receipt, which you must not lose.

I have mixed views on betting shops. What I like about them is that they force you to hand over real money at the counter, kind of like armed robbery in reverse. And there's nothing more stark than seeing your money vanish, possibly never to return. There's also the possibility of winning your bet in the office, or going back to collect at the counter. It's a nice feeling to see the cashier count your money like a bank teller and then pass it over. My golden rule if that ever happens is to leave the building immediately! Don't give it back to them.

Sometimes I find betting shops quite depressing places, lightened up only a touch since the introduction of the smoking ban. At ten thirty in the morning, betting shops are so fresh, radiating hope and the possibility of riches beyond our wildest dreams, before disintegrating into a paper-strewn mess, with a lot of anxious individuals chewing the mini-pens and gambling on everything in sight. A visit to the betting shop should be like a visit to the bank. Know your price before you go, do your business and get out.

Of course, the decent thing about the bookie's is that you can watch the races. And you can scream, because you can smell the inflammable tension in every shop, which allows you to let go a bit. After tipping Indian Pace to win the 2008 Galway Hurdle, I slipped into a Paddy Power office to watch the drama unfold. As Indian Pace came from behind to win at 11/1 (morning price), I was booming in the shop "*Come on the Indian!*" making an elderly gentleman completely exasperated as he waved his stick at me, beckoning me to stop.

Betting shops are for bank business or for shouting. From my experience, any other sojourn in a bookie's is time spent losing hard currency. And when you consider that around 85% of Paddy Power's Irish shop business is on horses and dogs, too many people are hanging about.

## The Phone

You can also do it on the phone, which I like, because instead of wasting time at the bookie's and getting involved in horse races that you shouldn't after a cursory and ineffectual glance at the *Racing Post*, if you are making the effort to ring to place a bet, you have probably already made up your mind as to your course of action. However, a bet on the phone can sometimes be dangerous for the undisciplined, in that a murmured "Put twenty on it for me, please, at the price, Nadine" can easily turn into a "Two hundred on the nose and make mine a double" in the seconds when you are listening to the hold music – but that's where I refer you, House of Commons style, to the fundamentals I gave you some moments ago.

Doing it on the phone is good clean fun and over quickly. A bit like teenagers canoodling in the cinema.

## Online Betting

We next turn to the beast that is online betting. The new pornography, I hear you say – perhaps, but the beauty of online gambling is its accessibility. The one downside I have with internet betting is the regulation of bets. It's often easier to place a large bet on a horse race in person or on the phone, than it is with an online bookmaker that is paranoid about getting taken to the cleaners. An online bookmaker can set a limit on how much you can place on an event. You may fancy a horse on form alone and not be involved in any kind of 'inside gamble' or 'touch' on the horse, but you may not be able to get as much money on the animal as you would like, especially at the smaller meetings. That's another reason why traditional online bookmakers are facing competition from the democratic exchange companies, such as Betfair, where the liquidity is determined by the punters themselves (who bet against each other rather than with the bookmakers) and where the punter can place a huge stake on an outcome if there is somebody willing to take it in the market. Anyway, we'll talk about exchanges later.

The appeal of online betting is in the clear choices which are presented to you. Every sport is neatly accessible, with hundreds of markets on offer and clever marketing to boot. It's completely anonymous. In a click you can place the desired bet at the desired odds. Online gambling is the perfect accompaniment to your TV set, as you can bet from the comfort of your living room as you watch the action. Online is also the place to be if you wish to bet 'in-running' – that is betting solely for markets that are 'in-play' – i.e. a football match that has started or a tennis match that is in progress.

## The Track

Aren't the races great altogether! I really enjoy arriving at the races and my main motivation for attending is to experience the live element. When I go to Cheltenham, I am working, so I am 'in the zone'. I don't let a drink pass my lips at Cheltenham. I'm constantly working and looking for angles. When I go socially to a race meeting, it's a different story. The objective when I attend socially is to enjoy myself, not necessarily to make a profit. And that's where a lot of mistakes are made, because people think they can easily do both.

There are traditional bookmakers who have a fixed presence at racetracks in the halls, but it's much more fun to bet with the 'rails bookmakers', as they are in closest proximity to the action. Years ago, I used to walk around the ring 'Columbo-style' for fifteen minutes before each race and watch the fluctuations in price, looking for an edge as I picked up 9/1 with one bookmaker on a horse that was 8/1 everywhere else. The convenience of using your phone, or going online, or using your phone to go online has curbed such behaviour, but the rails bookies still have their uses, especially if you want to get a good amount of money on a nag. It still carries a degree of mystique. The rails bookies work on a basis of hierarchy, with the big guns straddling the main enclosures at racecourses. What is important to be aware of with rails bookmakers is their each-way terms. Some rails bookies at racecourses are miserly with their each-way offerings, and play strictly by the letter of the law and not the spirit of racing and betting, to benefit themselves rather than the customers. I heard recently of a rails bookmaker offering 1/6 (one sixth) the odds for a place at Aintree, which was nothing short of disgraceful. So ensure you are getting the proper bang for your buck. A race with between 5 and 7 runners should pay 1/4 (one quarter) the odds for 2 horses to be placed. A race with over 8 runners should pay 1/5 (one fifth) the odds for 3 horses to be placed. A 'handicap' race (we'll come to that later) with over 12 runners should pay 1/4 the odds for a place, and a handicap with 16 runners or more should pay 1/4 the odds for 4 places rather than the usual 3. Off-course bookmakers often offer much better each-way terms than the rails bookies, so it's something to bear in mind.

What's killing racing in my mind from the betting perspective is the lack of options available to the punter at the course compared with staying at home and betting online. At home, I can see the market moves 10 minutes before the race (which is crucial, especially on the exchanges, as Betfair *is* the market for many meetings), watch interviews with connections on the television and get a proper look at the *Racing Post* online. If I go to the track, I need to have all that work done in advance; otherwise I am going to the bar.

Aside from the rails bookies, the other method for betting at the races is the **Tote,** where racegoers invest individually into a pool which pays an individual dividend after each race to the holders of winning bets on that race, subject to deductions of around 20%. Think of it as a sweepstake. The Tote is good if you want to have very small amounts on a race – and it can offer a much bigger price on an outsider than the bookmaker who is working to engineer a profit margin on his odds. When I backed Idole First to win at Cheltenham in 2005, he paid 33/1 on my accumulator, but 45/1 when I backed him on the Tote. For £20 each way, it made a significant difference. A horse called Ilnamar, who won the 2002 Coral Cup at Cheltenham at 25/1, paid 92/1 on the Tote. The most popular Tote bets are the **Placepot**, where you have to pick horses to be placed in the first 6 races on the card – and the **Jackpot**, where you need to find the winner of races 3, 4, 5 and 6 in Ireland and the first 6 races on the card in England. You can select more than 1 horse in each leg of the Placepot or Jackpot – so for example, in the Jackpot, if you select 3 horses in leg 1 (race 3), 2 horses in leg 2, 1 horse in leg 3 (1 horse only is nicknamed 'a banker') and 4 horses in leg 4, that equates to (3 X 2 X 1 X 4) = 24 X stake. The Jackpot pool pays to a €1 stake, but you can invest in 10-cent combinations if you want.

On the Wednesday at Punchestown in 2010, I had the winner of the big race, 16/1 chance Planet of Sound in the Jackpot. However, I didn't have the winners of 2 other legs, which was unfortunate as the 1 winner of the pool won €89,000 for an outlay of €64. I think the Jackpot is a fantastic bet, and I wish it was marketed more.

## Odds and Ends

Before you walk through the doors of any turf accountant (i.e. bookmaker) or racecourse, or browse a soccer market, an explanation of odds is important.

A 4 to 1 shot (5.0 in decimals) means that an outcome is likely to happen once in every 5 hypothetical runnings of the event. Odds which are quoted in fractions include your stake as part of the fraction, so if you place €25 on a winning 4/1 shot, you receive €125 back (€100 plus your stake of €25). 4/1 is classified as 'odds against', so 4 are the odds against your stake of 1. 'Odds on' is the opposite, so odds of 4/1 on (denoted as 1/4) are very short odds. So if you place €25 on a winning 1/4 shot, you receive €31.25 back (€6.25 plus your stake of €25). Mathematically, a 1/4 shot has an 80% chance of winning.

Odds offered by a traditional bookmaker are called 'fixed odds', in that you know what the potential return is, depending on your outlay.

When making the 'book' for a sporting event, the bookmaker frames the odds mathematically in order to make a profit in the long run. So if there are 10 runners in a horse race, and all of them are priced up at 9/1, or 10.0 in decimal terms, then each runner would have a 10% chance of winning. If the bookmaker takes an equal amount of €10 on each horse, he will break even, as 10.0 X 10 runners is 100% and that is classified as a 'round book'. If the bookmaker were to scratch his head, change his mind and offer only 8/1 on all of the runners, or 9.0 in decimal terms – and if an equal amount of €10 was once again wagered on each horse, the bookmaker would receive 10 units and pay out only 9, with the probability of each horse winning changing from 10% to 11.11%. The extra unit is 11.1% and if you multiply that by the number of runners, you get what is called an 'over-round' book of 111%. The bookmaker will thus make a profit on that race of €10, or 10% of turnover (11.1/111).

Complicated, innit? Not really. Just remember that like any casino, the odds are framed in favour of the house. If your image of a bookmaker is a gentleman puffing a fat cigar who has a big car which splashes you with mud at the bus stop, it's not because everyone who enters a bookmakers is dumb. It's because the house always wins. In practice, this is obviously an inexact science e.g. if a massive gamble is landed on a horse that starts at 10/1 and is then backed down in the market by punters into 3/1 and subsequently wins, then an individual bookmaker may be in trouble. But these things average out, and Irish bookmakers make an average net profit of between 2-5% on turnover. For the first half of 2010, Irish bookmaker Paddy Power made a profit of €52 million from a turnover of €1.8 billion. They made €18 million on the World Cup alone and that was a World Cup in which the favourites, Spain, won.

Bookmakers not only frame odds mathematically, they have their own experts and compilers in each sport with opinions and information on outcomes. This is where we get into a battle of wits. They work very hard to make money, so why don't you? That's why betting for 'a bit of interest' is the same thing in my view as taking a lighter to your fiver. To get the best odds, you must shop around. You should pay no loyalty to Paddy Power, Ladbrokes, Boylesports, Chronicle, William Hill or Hacketts. They have no loyalty to you and the only thing that should concern you is striking the best bargain for yourself, which means getting the best price. Some bookmakers such as Paddy Power have to be applauded for their punter-friendly stance and money-back specials, but I really don't care about all that if I can get a better price elsewhere.

To give an example, I was interested in a horse called Lady Lupus in the 2010 Irish Oaks, owned and trained by Aidan O'Brien and to be ridden by his son Joseph. Lady Lupus was 200/1 with one bookmaker and 100/1 with others. I put €10 each way on Lady Lupus at 200/1 and the filly finished third. So if I had an account with only one bookmaker and placed that bet at 100/1, I would have received only €260, rather than the €510 I collected.

Promiscuity is a good thing when it comes to bookmakers. The competitive nature of the internet has given greater value to punters – so by having sites like **www.oddschecker.com** and **www.easyodds.com,** one can compare in real time the odds of every single online bookmaker for a certain event, with serious fluctuations in price, depending on the opinion of the bookmaker.

## The Market

The market is where the action resides. It's essential to have your finger on the pulse of market moves in betting, because people with a lot more money than you, some of them bookmakers themselves, or big punters, determine the market by helping to move the prices by activity. For example, a golf tournament may be priced up on a Monday, and depending on the weight of money on a certain player, or tipster advice, the market may move in a player's favour. The market may also move against the player, if he announces he has a sore wrist or has sacked his caddie. Bookmakers examine their liabilities in detail, and trade against these liabilities to ensure a profit. There's no point in a bookie having the best price on Tiger Woods in a golf tournament and then taking in an avalanche of money on Woods unless a) they are making him the biggest price in the industry for a good reason known only to themselves, or b) they are prepared to hedge some of that money in the market by backing Woods themselves to reduce their exposure. Ahead of a World Cup, there may be a flood of patriotic money for England, which sees their price contract, but the bookmaker might be happy to take this money and then trim the price even further to precipitate a bandwagon effect. This happens when all punters follow the Pied Piper in the form of a tumbling market and become emotionally involved.

I remember going to the greyhounds at Shelbourne Park in Dublin as a teenager and there was a big bookie, the king of the ring as it were. He priced up only two dogs from the six runners in the race and was bellowing gobbledegook which I couldn't understand. The only thing I was interested in as a regular attendee was sausage and chips and how a mechanical hare could fool the dogs every time. However, I noticed his unusual method of not pricing up every dog. He roared something into the night sky and half of the punters in the ring surged towards him, taking a better price on one of the dogs than was on offer elsewhere in the ring. He was playing the game – and neither of the two dogs won. I never checked if he was taking bets on the other runners, but if he was luring people into a lemming mentality, it worked.

The market plays its most important role in horse-racing. A race at Wolverhampton may be worth only £3,000 to the winner, but there may be up to £1 million traded on it on Betfair, the betting exchange, which is the focus of the next chapter. Betfair is the *de facto* market for a lot of horse-racing, and the rails bookies will reflect that in their prices. At a big meeting like Cheltenham, the off-course shops and rails bookies can influence the market, but a horse drifting alarmingly on Betfair, close to the beginning of a race, must be monitored. Somebody always knows something, so that's why it's wise, especially for smaller race meetings, to keep your powder dry until you see the market moves, both on the morning of the race, and then just before the race.

Tipsters such as Tom Segal in the *Racing Post* have a fantastic reputation, so their selections ahead of big meetings will always cause the bookies to slim their prices. It may rain heavily, and that may cause your horse to shorten or drift in price, or a connection (trainer or owner) may appear on the television and express dizzy confidence or complete pessimism before the off, altering the market. Stick to your guns and have the courage of your convictions – after all, it's your opinion that counts, but the more you are 'in the know', the better your chance. In advance of the 2010 Cheltenham Festival, I noticed that top English trainer Paul Nicholls, who is a very honest and open man, was raving about the chances of his horse Sanctuaire in the juvenile hurdle. Nicholls had three champions in Kauto Star, Master Minded and Big Buck's in his team that week, but still highlighted this French-bred youngster. Sanctuaire was backed off the boards from 7/1 into 4/1 and stormed home an easy winner.

You must also examine the ownership of the runner that is being backed in the market. In 2002, Mini Sensation was an 18/1 shot on the morning of the Welsh Grand National. Trained by Jonjo O'Neill, he was ridden by Tony Dobbin and down the bottom of the weights. A poor fourth on his previous outing, Mini Sensation was nevertheless subject to a huge gamble, starting at 8/1 and winning well. His owner was legendary punter JP McManus, who has pulled off some fantastic coups over the years. His green, white and gold colours are synonymous with jumps racing, so when the money is down for one of JP's, or a horse from any other owner or yard that is respected, then it's worth reading between the lines.

## Value

You may often hear tipsters describe something as a 'value bet'. Of course it is only a value bet if it wins, but the whole point of value is that you are comparing your opinion with that of the bookmakers on price, which theoretically will guarantee you a profit if you are right more times than they are. A lot of professional gamblers recommend that you compile your own book against the bookmaker to estimate if you have spotted value. Compiling a book is called 'making a tissue'.

So for example, if there is a 5-horse race, the bookmaker may price up the horses as follows:

A: 6/4 – 2.5 (100 / 2.5) = 40%

B: 9/4 – 3.25 (100 / 3.25) = 30.77%

C: 7/2 – 4.5 (100 / 4.5) = 22.22%

D: 9/1 – 10 (100 / 10) = 10%

E: 20/1 – 21 (100 / 21) = 4.76%

The percentages quoted reflect the chance of each horse winning. That would give a bookmaker an over-round book of 107.75%.

Now, without looking at the bookmaker prices, and using your knowledge, you estimate that the chances of each horse are as follows:

A: 2/1 = 33.33%

B: 11/4 = 26.67%

C: 7/2 = 22.22%

D: 6/1 = 14.29%

E: 25/1 = 3.85%

You have the view that the two favourites are too short in the betting, so backing them would not be reflective of their chances. But horse D is a 6/1 chance in your opinion, which makes it a value bet when compared to the bookmaker's 9/1.

Obviously, value is dependent on you having a better knowledge of the outcome than the bookmaker on each contest. Value also doesn't tell you what amount should be staked. The bookmakers construct a book on profit margins, but the opinions of their odds compilers also play a big part. So if you feel you have an edge on them in a particular market (i.e. Spanish football), then it would do you no harm to form a tissue.

## Ante-Post Betting

Let's talk about ante-post betting. Ante-post is where the bookmakers price up an event well in advance of its date. Better prices are generally on offer. This usually applies to horse-racing, i.e. Aintree Grand National prices at Christmas, well before the horses 'go to post'. Nowadays it applies to all sports – so for example, a bookmaker may provide a Champions League winner market in soccer in August, 9 months before the season ends. I have only had one proper ante-post bet in my life, on Turpin Green in the 2007 Cheltenham Gold Cup at 100/1 and I was lucky that he finished third.

My view on ante-post betting on horses is to forget about it, until a bookmaker goes 'Non-runner No Bet' before the race (you would get your money back if the horse was a non-runner). Non-runner No Bet is often introduced around 10 days before Cheltenham, or on the week of the Grand National. The trap with ante-post betting on racing is that you lose if the horse doesn't run. You could back a horse at 66/1 in October before Cheltenham and he may be favourite the week before the race. The horse may only be 2/1 on the week of the race, but your 66/1 voucher would become redundant if the horse was lame and declared a non-runner on the morning of the race. Also, not all horses can go on differing types of ground, so you are taking a big chance in that regard. Your horse may love a mud-bath, and then it could end up sunny and hard underfoot on the day, reducing his chance significantly.

I examined ante-post prices for some big races in 2010 and I was surprised to see little or no change that would make it more attractive for me to bet at any time other than on the day of the race. In January, Imperial Commander was 16/1 to win the Cheltenham Gold Cup and won on the day in March at 7/1. Binocular was 8/1 for the Champion Hurdle in January and won on the day at a bigger price of 9/1. Big Zeb was 10/1 in January to win the Champion Chase and was also 10/1 on the day. Big Buck's was 4/6 to win the World Hurdle in January and 5/6 on the day. Don't Push It was 40/1 to win the Aintree Grand National in February, but was that price until the week of the race, and went to post at 18/1 on Betfair. So you get my drift.

In horse-racing, you need to have all things on your side. Ante-post bets on horse-racing are in the bookmakers' favour. There are two reasons punters do them: a) for the prospect of a large profit if it all comes off, and b) to trade, which means that they may back a horse at 20/1 for Cheltenham in November and then 'lay it off' (or take a bet on the same horse on an exchange) at 2/1 in February to make a profit regardless of the result. I will talk about exchanges in the next chapter, but it's dangerous to offer odds and take bets in an ante-post market, because how do you know that your information is 100% accurate? Some poor soul offered 999/1 on Betfair on Kicking King winning the 2005 Cheltenham Gold Cup after trainer Tom Taaffe ruled out the horse because of a respiratory infection. Kicking King had been at the top of the market, and when the horse surprised Taaffe by showing his good health at the yard, the trainer had a change of mind and declared the horse to run. Kicking King won easily on the day at 4/1, making £25,000 from a £25 bet for one lucky punter and causing similar liabilities for another gentleman.

Soccer can offer gems of value in the ante-post market, especially as you know that the teams will turn up to play! Some value bets you could have had in soccer markets if you knew your apples from oranges in 2010 were: Inter Milan at 14/1 to win the Champions League before the last 16; Atletico Madrid at 33/1 to win the Europa League in February; Didier Drogba at 9/2 to win the Premier League Golden Boot in January (when Chelsea were odds-on to win the title); 7/2 on Tottenham to finish in the top 4 of the table in January.

## Spread Betting

I cannot pen a book on sports betting without talking about spread betting. Betting involves risk – and the extent of that risk is contingent on how much you are willing to bet. At least with fixed-odds betting you know the potential win/loss will not change depending on the result. With spread betting, the risks and rewards are heightened. How does it work?

A spread-betting bookmaker, e.g. Sporting Index, makes predictions on various markets – and you, the punter, bet against that prediction. So if Ireland are playing Scotland in the Six Nations, and it's going to be a wet day in Dublin, the spread-betting firm may estimate that the total number of points may be between 29 and 32. Spread betting tests your accuracy, as you either have to 'sell 29', which means you think the total number of points will be below 29, or you have to 'buy 32', which means you believe the total number of points will be above 32. It's a bit like Bruce Forsyth's card game, when he used to say "Highaaa" or "Lowaaa" in a mildly amusing fashion. So let's say I think the rugby game is going to be based on penalty kicks in the rain and I predict Ireland will beat Scotland 15-9. Therefore I would sell the total points at 29. The profit or loss on spread betting depends on a) the accuracy of your prediction, and b) your stake. It doesn't matter who wins or loses the game, because that's not what the bet relates to. So if I sell 29 points for €10, and the result is 12-6 in favour of Scotland, I win the difference of the total points (29 − 18 = 11 X my stake of €10 = €110). On the other hand, if the game turns out to be a high-scoring affair and Ireland win 28-22, that would total 50 points and by selling at 29 I would lose 21 times my stake, or €210. If I bought the spread at 32 and the score was 28-22, I would win 18 times my stake, or €180. So you can see that the amount you stake can have a huge impact on what you win or lose. Imagine you lost 21 times €50 on one event. Therefore, some spread-betting firms put a stop on how much you can actually win or lose on a particular event.

Another example of a spread bet is a long-term market. As I write this, in late 2010, Chelsea are 40-43 in the Champions League outright market with Sporting Index. Where there is more than one team, the market is divided into points for finishing positions, so for instance in the long-term Champions League market, the winner is allotted 100 points, the runner-up is given 75 points, the losing semi-finalists are given 50 points, the losing quarter-finalists are handed 25 points and the losing last 16 teams receive 10 points. If I take a strong view that Chelsea will do well and buy them at 43 for €5, and if Chelsea lose in the final, I will win (75 − 43 X 5) = €160. However, if Chelsea mess up and lose their last 16 game, I lose (10 − 43 X 5) = €165.

If you want to spread bet, I advise you to play for fun at first, as you will need to be very accurate in your predictions, and adopt a conservative mindset to staking. Even the best tipsters can get it terribly wrong sometimes. And my overall advice in this book is to forsake risk for profit.

# Chapter 4

*Laying*

There's a friend of mine, a football expert, who has an encyclopaedic knowledge of the beautiful game. In his first full year of betting he made €25,000 on soccer bets. No word of a lie. We'll call this gentleman Mr Crocodile. I have a problem with Mr Crocodile, and the problem is that for a man with a brilliant loaf, he doesn't open his mind to all of the options on the table in terms of making money in soccer betting. I have tried to explain the 'L' word to him, but to date, I have failed. We're not talking about love either. Maybe it's my garbled turn of phrase, or religious zeal that puts him off. I have attempted to softly bring terms like 'internet betting exchanges' into the conversation, as his demeanour improves with a cold beer in hand, but to no avail. Mr Crocodile, like the ancient reptile he is, is resistant to change when it comes to prey. He may be a killing machine, but his method is from a bygone age. And when one's *modus operandi* is limited, one may get into a monotonous routine, and one may not fully enjoy the potential bounty on offer. This species of Crocodile could add a lot more to his diet. So I want to preach like a Baptist to you all, because I have devoted a chapter to this one word: *Laying*.

Playing on the exchanges, or backing and laying, is something you need to know if you want to make money on sports betting. It's my fervent belief that laying has not pricked the consciousness of many gamblers and they are at an immediate disadvantage. The bookmakers have done a great job at keeping this 21st Century concept hidden from massive consumption.

What is laying? Laying is playing the bookie, or opposing an outcome. How many times have you argued with a friend over a football match? It may be Liverpool v Manchester United at Anfield. Your friend is convinced United will win. You are convinced United won't win. Maybe you are both going to watch the match on a Sunday afternoon down the pub. If you both strike a bet, where you, in your absolute certainty that you are onto a winner, offer your United-loving friend a price of 2/1 that they won't win at Anfield, he may take the bait and give you a tenner. So you've both, probably without thinking too much about it, engaged in backing and laying, where a bet is matched between the pair of you. And that's exactly how betting exchanges operate. You have decided to 'lay' United at 2/1, or 3.0 in decimal terms. If United win, you have to give your friend back €30 (a profit of €20 plus the €10 stake). If Liverpool win or if it's a draw, then your friend loses his tenner.

The oldest and by far the biggest exchange, after a hat-tip to Betdaq and WBX, is Betfair. Betfair has done to betting what aviation did to transport. Betfair is an ingenious concept, in that the exchange, which acts as facilitator and regulator, makes commission of around 5% on every winning transaction. For every backer, there is a layer, so for every transaction, there is a winner and a loser. Unlike the traditional bookies, with exchanges it's person to person betting. Betfair gives a punter a lot to think about.

'Backing' in traditional terms is attractive on an exchange, as Betfair is unlike the bookmakers, who are working to strict profit targets on turnover per event. Remember the over-round? On an exchange, your bookie is just as likely to be a punter like you, so that punter may offer much better odds, because he/she is certain in his/her mind that the result will not occur. For example, my biggest-priced-ever winner of a sporting event came in the 2004 Tucson Open, when golfer Heath Slocum won at 140/1. I had €10 on his shoulders on Betfair. He was only 80/1 with the bookmakers. Some poor fella or dolly was willing to lay Slocum at that price and they got stung.

We all know, though, what backing is. "Who did you back?" How often do we say that to our friend at the races or in the office? I've never heard anybody say to me: "Who did you lay?" And folks, you are missing out. Big time. I think in part this is a result of our innate psychology. We all want to back a winner, see our judgement vindicated, gain a financial reward, and tell everyone about it. Backing a horse to lose may not generate the same emotional response, when the horse trails in seventh. "Lose, lose, come on, lose!" – it doesn't have the same ring to it, does it?

I bring you back to the most powerful word in this game: *profit*. Isn't the whole point to make money? If you can make more money over time by laying rather than backing, then be proud of your ability to lay – and celebrate it.

You may be thinking at this point, "But how much do I win?" You win the amount for which you lay the bet. So if you lay a 5/1 shot for €10 and it loses, you win €10 minus commission. In laying, you decide how much you win, subject to market liquidity and the lay being a successful one.

Remember, laying is stating that an event won't happen. Let me give you another example. On his return to golf after his off-course activities changed his life irrevocably, Tiger Woods teed it up at the Masters in 2010. He'd previously won the tournament four times, but for me, he was never, ever going to win this time. He had not played competitively since November 2009, and there is a big difference between practice rounds and the heat of competition in a major championship. I expected him to do well, but not to win. In the early stages of the third round, he was hovering around the leaderboard, but I'd seen too many loose shots and too many lapses in concentration from someone who was obviously rusty. So I pressed the 'lay' button on Betfair for €100. I thought my money was safe as houses, and so it proved. The odds I offered were 4/1, although on Betfair they are expressed in decimals, so in this case, 5.0. So if Woods had won, I would have owed the exchange €400, just as a bookie does when you back a 4/1 winner at the track. The fact that anyone was willing to back Woods at 4/1 gave me confidence, as I believed I was dealing with punters on the other side of the market who were either more greedy or less informed than me. When I lay, I often capitalise on the psychological avarice of a gambler who is more interested in getting a better price than whether the outcome will actually occur.

Laying is all about having balls of steel. Remember you are the bookie. It can be quite easy to lay a load of losers. For example, there may be fifteen runners in a horse race. It's much easier to pick a loser than a winner, and on probability, when you lay a horse in the race at 9/1, you have a good chance, with fourteen other runners on your side. If you lay a horse for €10 at 9/1, you are exposing yourself for €90 if the horse wins. Other than that 9/1 shot, it doesn't matter which horse wins the race. A 100/1 shot could win, but it's completely irrelevant to the bet you have taken. Unlike the traditional bookmaker, you don't have to lay every horse in the race and the amount you win is fixed by the amount you lay minus commission. The amount you lose depends on the stated liability if the horse you lay wins.

On an exchange, there is a little table of back odds and lay odds and the money which is available in the market to back and lay at those odds. The money is a total of all the orders placed at the particular odds on the screen by punters who wish to either back or lay. On Betfair, the punters set the odds. So if I want to back Horse A at the Curragh at 7.5 for €10, but he's only available at 5.5, I have to wait until someone 'matches' my bet, or decides to lay me at that price. My bet waits in a queue until it is taken, or not taken. I can cancel it if I want, or allow it to go to the in-play market for when the race starts.

So to go back to our original example, on Sunday morning there may be €4,000 in the 2/1 bracket available to lay Manchester United. The €4,000 is the total sum of all the money that various punters wish to back United at that price. On the exchange, the odds are shown as 3.0. If you, the Liverpool fan, had €1,000 in your account, you could lay United up to a total of €500. Of course, you don't have to lay your entire account – in fact, it would be crazy to do so. A sensible option would be to lay for €20 and build your bank up slowly over time.

My opening exchanges on what punters call 'The Machine' (Betfair) were of the hair-raising variety. This was back in 2003 again. I decided to start laying horses and see how far I could go. The first horse I layed was a winner, so I was immediately down a good bit of cash. I then proceeded to lay 38 successive losers, making a tidy sum. I never got hit. And that made me think that it was easy. Greed was taking over and a fall was imminent. Eventually the hits would come. It's funny how you remember the names. Hugs Dancer was a horse I layed for a significant amount at 5/1 in a flat race. I was so high with the breadth of my wins that I was not conducting proper research. And when you get hit, there is no hiding place, when you owe your stake times x – and that could amount to a lot, depending on your exposure.

The critical error that I made in the early days on Betfair was not to withdraw my funds on a regular basis if I won, reverting to an original bank. I also had this annoying and fatal habit of laying my entire account to build up cash rapidly. My account turned into a black hole, as I would build up money, lay a loser and lose, and then deposit again. I got out of that habit with haste. So two basics on the exchange are: a) withdraw regularly, and b) never lay more than half of your account. Clever stockbrokers don't expose themselves. Why should you?

The good news is that we are here on the planet to learn. I have had only two losing years at Cheltenham on the radio since my first foray in 2002. In 2006 and 2010, my tipping was brutal, but on both occasions I personally left Gloucestershire with more money than I had arrived with, even if it wasn't cash in hand. All of this was down to laying. In 2010, I carefully layed twelve horses to lose and didn't get hit once. The stakes were all small, and taking into account the losing 'backs' I came out with a profit of €208. I have preached patience before. The exchanges require *extreme* patience.

The exchanges are powerful beasts because they carry such transparent liquidity and move by the second. In-running betting on an exchange like Betfair is an industry in itself. This is where backing and laying continues for all 90 minutes of a soccer match, or for the entire duration of the Grand National. Those with big money back odds-on shots for a small, but in their eyes, certain profit, but there can be massive fluctuations as a sporting event ebbs and flows. A lot of traditional bookmakers and City types use exchanges, on the racecourse and off it. An average UK race on Betfair will see between £750,000 and £1 million matched. The biggest ever amount matched on a soccer match (including in-running) was €38 million, when Switzerland beat Spain in a group game at the 2010 World Cup. In the early days I went through my phase of playing the exchanges in a silly manner. Now, as a Tottenham Hotspur fan, I think they are the best thing since Harry Redknapp.

However, there are horror stories. Golden Silver won a Chase at Fairyhouse back in April 2010. Unfortunately when a horse falls at the track, his price immediately goes to 1000 – or 999/1 on Betfair. That is the maximum price available to back on the exchange, and 1.01 (or 1/100) is the minimum price to lay. Golden Silver's silks are red, and another horse in the race also wore red silks. The on-course commentator made a mistake, as we all do, and said that Golden Silver had fallen, when he hadn't. So some greedy clown layed Golden Silver at 1000 on Betfair and was stung for 5 figures. Such is the danger of betting on horses in-running.

As far as I am concerned, unless you have one of those CIA laptops, to bet in-running on racing is a dangerous game, especially as so much is done on the rails at the racecourses. Even in golf, the TV pictures are ever so slightly behind the action out on the course and the prices change on the exchange before you know what has happened. I was going up the walls at the 2010 Memorial Tournament having placed €25 on Justin Rose to win at 84/1, wondering if I should trade out and get some money back, as his price was see-sawing before the TV cameras would show what actually happened. As he was winning, I didn't want to lay him until I was certain he was going to lose. So I held out and it paid off as he won. A 999/1 horse can actually win, as backers of a Tony McCoy ridden horse called Family Business discovered in a chase at Southwell in 2002. Family Business fell. McCoy remounted – which you are allowed to do – and then the horses in front of him fell. Family Business won the race. McCoy's opportunism gave him the most unlikely of victories and national news coverage. In soccer, Wigan were 2-0 down at home to Arsenal with 10 minutes to go in their Premier League game before the end of the 2009-10 season. Wigan then proceeded to score three times after being available at 799/1 at one stage on Betfair. Of course, it was a one-in-a-million day, but who would be a layer at that price?

What is attractive for a punter who bets in-running on a horse race is that he may take the view that a favourite will produce his best work in the second half of a race. The favourite may have been 6.0 at the off, or 5/1, and the punter could decide to ask to back it at 25.0 during the race. Betfair always matches horses at the best price, so the punter could end up with a much better price in-running than he ordered, if his horse struggled in-running and someone else made a move on that basis. In 2006, Noland won the Supreme Novices' Hurdle at Cheltenham having been way off the pace at halfway. Noland went off at 7.0, but was available at 1000 in-running and ended up storming up the hill to win on the line. A punter requested a much lower price to back, but Betfair gave him the best price on offer by matching him at 1000. That was a very costly lay for the imbecile who offered 999/1.

Another way to make money on an exchange is to trade. I like my golf betting and there are plenty of trades on offer in golf. What an exchange allows you to do is back an outcome and then lay it back at a better price, making a profit for yourself whatever the final result. So, for example, if you backed golfer Louis Oosthuizen to win the 2010 Open Championship at 450 on Betfair for €20, you would be looking at a return of around €8,550 after commission, if Oosthuizen won. Oosthuizen may have been part of a portfolio of bets, whereby you invested a total of €200 on the tournament. Of course, Oosthuizen did win, but let's say in theory that his price was cut to 5.0 on the exchange, or 4/1. You could then lay Oosthuizen back at 4/1 for €1,000. That would cut your maximum profit to €4,370, but would guarantee you a profit of €800, regardless of the eventual outcome of the tournament.

You can also lay to back. For example, if you think a horse which is 2/1 will drift in-running, but would like to back it in-running at a better price, you could lay the horse for €200 at 3.0, and then if it goes out to 5/1 in running, you could back it for €100 at that price (6.0), making €100 on the race regardless, because you have completed a successful trade.

There's one final area of the exchanges which the advanced punters become involved in, and that's **arbitrage**. The concept is that you back an outcome at a certain price with a traditional bookmaker and lay it off simultaneously with an exchange to guarantee a low-risk profit. So an Irish bookmaker may price up England to win Euro 2012 at 8/1, but an English exchange, which may have a client base of patriotic punters, may have England at odds of 6/1 to lay. So if I simultaneously back England for €100 at 8/1 (9.0) and lay them at 7.0 for €130, I am guaranteed a profit either way. If England win, I win (€800 – €780) = €20. If England lose, I win (the €130 I have layed minus 5% commission = €123.50 – €100) = €23.50. 'Arbing', as it is called, is for the professionals, but it is useful to know about it.

It may be troubling you as to how an ordinary person can act as a 'bookie', taking bets on horses. Well, in most normal bookmakers, you are given the option of betting on something not to happen, i.e. Tiger Woods not to win a major in 2010 at 5/4. In effect, if you do that, you are 'laying Tiger Woods to win a major'. So laying is just another way of backing something not to happen. The exchange (i.e. Betfair) is the licensed bookmaker and the one which pays tax, takes public money and manages the market. So start laying!

# Chapter 5

## *Understanding Horse-Racing*

When I was small, there was an amusement arcade in Bray, Co Wicklow which had a game called 'Derby Day'. Obviously it was for the unwitting, as I never seemed to win. There were eight horses, all paying out different amounts, so if you picked horse Number 1 in red, you would win 20p. (Remember the 1986 gold 20p pieces?) Number 1 won most of the races. If you managed to have your 10p on Number 8 on one of the rare occasions he was first up the mechanical track, you would collect over two punts. Real horse-racing is built on the same foundations. Some horses are favourites in the betting and some are outsiders. A favourite is denoted as F, i.e. 2/1F.

Before we examine the do's and don'ts of the sport of kings, it may be a good idea to understand it. I don't feel the need to explain the rules of soccer or Gaelic games. These are highly popular sports for many reasons – the fact they are easily understood is certainly not a hindrance. Horse-racing is a minority sport in Ireland and the UK, but it remains the greatest generator of turnover for bookmakers. One million people attend Irish race meetings each year at our 26 racecourses, so while horse-racing has experienced its fair share of difficulties in recent times, Ireland remains at the head of the market when it comes to success, breeding and prize money.

Horse-racing is the clearest example of a sport where the supporters of it truly understand it and those who are not fans know little or nothing about it. You may go to the races socially, pick a name you might like, or rely on me or somebody more astute for tips, but all the information is all out there, and once you have a rudimentary knowledge, then you can make up your own mind. It makes it all the more satisfying if you can work it out for yourself. That's what making money is about, how *your* expertise made the difference. My belief is that racing is quite daunting to analyse for a lot of people, so they just don't go there. Cricket is not too dissimilar. I could happily sit down and watch a test match for hours, because I understand the nature of the sport and I'm a patient man. Others may find the elongated exchanges of cricket boring, but you cannot say that about horse-racing, where the longest race, the Aintree Grand National, takes an average of 9 minutes. Races on the flat over the minimum trip of 5 furlongs can last just under a minute, confirming your fate faster than a lap of a Formula One track. The waiting at race meetings is for the next race, as it takes 30 minutes for each to be run.

So here we go. This is my attempt at explaining the nags, the four-legged animals that break into our consciousness a few times a year, or maybe a few times a day depending on your disposition.

## Flat and National Hunt

There are two types of horse-racing – flat and National Hunt (or jumps) racing. The flat season is traditionally held from May to November, with the jumps season running from November until April.

Flat racing revolves around young thoroughbreds, which begin racing as young as two, generally peak at three – and then are retired to breed. Some flat horses continue to race, but the majority of them produce their best work up to the age of five. A male flat horse is called a colt, a female is called a filly. The thoroughbred's lineage goes back to around 1700 from a small pool of Anglo/Arabian stallions, which had more speed than the traditional animal.

Flat racing is big business, as stud farms can command huge fees for the offspring of a top stallion. The 2001 Epsom and Irish Derby winner Galileo is an example of a leading stallion and the brilliant Sea the Stars, who was unbeaten as a three-year-old in 2009, is expected to do well at stud. So the life of a stallion is pretty neat, if you think about it.

Flat racing has been dominated by a few distinct figures in recent times, such as Sheikh Mohammed bin Rashid Al Maktoum, ruler of the United Arab Emirates, who is behind the Godolphin breeding and racing organisation and John Magnier with his Coolmore operation in Ballydoyle, County Tipperary, where the horses are trained by Aidan O'Brien. Magnier helped to establish the Irish breeding Goliath with his late father-in-law, Vincent O'Brien, undoubtedly the greatest trainer racing has ever seen. Vincent, or MV as he was known, saddled the winner of the Champion Hurdle and the Gold Cup at Cheltenham three years running, trained the winner of the Aintree Grand National three years running with three different horses and then became a flat trainer, winning everything on offer, including six Epsom Derbies and the Prix de l'Arc de Triomphe, which is effectively the European Flat Championship. Flat racing has no obstacles (obviously) and races are run from stalls over distances from 5 furlongs (there are 8 furlongs to a mile) up to 2½ miles. All five English 'Classics' – the most prestigious races – can only be contested by three-year-olds. The Classics are the 2,000 Guineas (a race over a mile for colts); the 1,000 Guineas (a race over a mile for fillies); the Derby (a race over 1½ miles for colts and fillies); the Oaks (a race over 1½ miles for fillies); and the St Leger (a race over 1³/₄ miles for colts and fillies). There are Irish and English versions of the five Classics, but the Irish St Leger is different from the rest in that there is no barrier to age.

The last horse to win the Triple Crown of the English 2,000 Guineas at Newmarket, the Derby at Epsom and the St Leger at Doncaster was Nijinsky in 1970. So he proved himself as the king at variable distances. Sea the

Stars, who was trained in Ireland by John Oxx, won the English 2,000 Guineas and the Epsom Derby, but skipped the St Leger to run in (and win) the Arc in Paris. The Arc is run over a mile and a half. What has to be noted about the Classics for flat horses is that each horse carries the same weight, so theoretically the best horse will be identified. Every horse in the Epsom Derby, which is the greatest flat race of them all, carries 9 stone, which consists of the jockey's weight plus lead in the saddle to reach 9 stone. A Classic race is designated as a 'Group' race, and all Group races – be they 1, 2, or 3 (with 1 the most valuable in terms of prize-money) – are level weights affairs.

A Handicap is another proposition altogether. A Handicap race is where every runner carries a different weight. The weights are decided by the official handicapper, employed by the racing authorities to give a rating to each horse in training. So Sea the Stars would have had by far the best rating of any flat horse, and if he had run in a handicap, he would have given a lot of weight away to his rivals, because the purpose of a handicap is to give each horse the same chance. Ratings are decided with a nod to past form, taking variables of distance into account. So if horse A carries 5 pounds more than horse B, then horse A is rated a better horse than B by 5 pounds, which in theory would mean that if horses A and B ran off level weights, horse A would beat horse B by 5 lengths. A length is the length of a horse, totalling about 8 feet, which is why you hear the distance of victory being called half a length, or a neck, or a short head. Handicaps apply to flat racing and jumps racing.

National Hunt, or jumps racing, consists of three elements: steeplechases, hurdle races and bumpers. National Hunt racing is for horses aged four or older, and most of them run until the age of twelve. As they will be tackling obstacles and won't be considered for breeding, males are castrated or in racing terms 'gelded'. Ouch. Gelding is used to steady a horse's temperament over jumps and prevent any amorous flights of fancy. Female horses in the jumps sphere are called mares. Most National Hunt races take place over at least 2 miles, with 4½ miles the maximum trip. In Ireland, most National Hunt horses start off in a 'bumper' which is a 2-mile flat race, to determine their ability. It's usually the last race on the card.

Some horses, especially those that are big in stature, begin their racing careers over fences, but most begin their obstacle-training over hurdles, which are usually 3 feet high. The idea of a hurdle race is to identify the most nimble jumpers at speed, which is why the Champion Hurdle at Cheltenham is run over 2 miles. Most top hurdle horses are in the five to eight age bracket. Some horses may be small, so they are not suited to the larger fences for steeplechasing. These fences can stretch to around 5 feet high, but can be less than that. The Grand National is a steeplechase, so too the Cheltenham Gold Cup. When horses mature, they can generally race at longer distances, which is why the winners of the Gold Cup over the trip of 3¼ miles tend to be aged between seven and nine, with Grand

National winners usually in the nine to eleven age bracket. Like the Epsom Derby, the Cheltenham Gold Cup is a race off level weights – known in National Hunt terms as a Grade 1, 2 or 3 race. The Irish and English Grand Nationals are handicaps, with weights ranging from 12 stone down to 10 stone. Horses which have not won a race over their chosen code (hurdle or chase) before the season starts are called novices. It is possible for novices to race against more experienced rivals – an example being Alderbrook, who won the Champion Hurdle in 1995 as a novice.

So who can we remember from National Hunt history and why? Golden Miller won the Gold Cup and the Grand National in the 1930s. Arkle beat the unbeatable Mill House en route to a hat trick of Cheltenham Gold Cups and routinely gave huge amounts of weight away in handicaps, but still won all before him. In the 1970s Red Rum was the first horse to win three Aintree Grand Nationals, and did it twice carrying top weight. Dawn Run, who was an Irish-trained mare, is the only horse to have won the 2-mile Champion Hurdle and the 3¼ mile Gold Cup at Cheltenham. Istabraq won three Champion Hurdles – and won them very easily. Moscow Flyer won the 2-mile Champion Chase at Cheltenham twice and was a brilliant jumper of a fence. Best Mate won a hat trick of Gold Cups. Kauto Star won the 3-mile King George Chase at Kempton on a right-handed, tight track four years running, landed two Cheltenham Gold Cups and won the Tingle Creek Chase over only 2 miles at Sandown.

Denman gave huge amounts of weight away but still won the Hennessy Gold Cup Chase at Newbury over 3¼ miles on two occasions. That's why these horses are special – because they have often won over varying distances and taken the best races on offer. Horses by breeding are built for certain distances. Moscow Flyer was not suited to racing over 3 miles, nor was Istabraq. One Man, who won the 1998 Champion Chase at Cheltenham, did not have the requisite stamina for the Gold Cup. In flat racing, this is even more pronounced. A horse that is bred for a mile usually cannot 'stay' a mile and a half. A horse which stays two miles doesn't have the speed to win a mile race. That's why it's important to have a look at the sire (the father) and the dam (the mother) of a flat horse. The sire may have been a sprinter, so will his son win a staying race?

When Sea the Stars became the first horse in twenty years to win the English 2000 Guineas over 1 mile and the Epsom Derby over 1½ miles, we had witnessed a very special horse, just like Nijinsky. Shergar won the Epsom Derby in 1981 by 10 lengths. That's what made him a freak. Sinndar was a great middle-distance flat horse, because of his visually impressive wins in the 2000 Epsom Derby and the Arc. And flat horses are often recalled for their amazing capabilities at stud. Sadler's Wells, the 1984 Irish 2000 Guineas winner, is easily the most prolific stallion. He was champion sire in Ireland and the UK fourteen times. Montjeu and Galileo were middle distance (1½ mile) champions, so their offspring are generally best at that distance.

Galileo is a son of Sadler's Wells, and the 2008 Epsom Derby winner, New Approach, is a son of Galileo.

For National Hunt, breeding is important, but less crucial. One area to note is the point-to-point arena, the rural steeplechasing over farmland where many future stars begin their careers. Cheltenham Gold Cup winner Best Mate won his point to point over 3 miles on heavy ground in Ireland, but when he lined up at 7/1 for the 2002 Gold Cup many had forgotten that as they questioned his stamina before the race. He won easily.

One more point about National Hunt. I think it has more popular appeal because it's more entertaining to the eye, but it also conjures a lot of human stories. For example, it's a realisable dream for a syndicate, if they are very lucky, to have a winner at Cheltenham, or for a small trainer to have a Grand National winner in his stable. Aintree Grand National Winner Monty's Pass in 2003 was trained by Jimmy Mangan in Cork and Silver Birch, the 2007 winner of the Grand National, was trainer Gordon Elliott's fourth winner in Britain!

There is huge money in breeding flat horses, so the flat is a hard-nosed business. Breeding takes precedence over racing. You just have to look at the dispute between Coolmore and Manchester United manager Alex Ferguson, over the stud rights to the horse, Rock of Gibraltar, to realise that. Jumps racing does have its big owners, like Michael O'Leary of Ryanair fame and JP McManus, but it's a more romantic sport, where a small Carlow trainer such as Tom Foley could send Danoli over to Cheltenham with the hopes of thousands of Irish punters on the horse's shoulders. After a barren opening day for the Irish at the Cheltenham Festival in 1994, Danoli won the first race on the second day. A heavily backed 7/4 favourite, Danoli's win was an emotional one, for the connections of the horse and the many strangers whose punting week depended on it.

## Ground & Temperament

When you walk on a hard road, as opposed to a muddy field, the walk is much quicker. Horses are delicate animals, and have legs comparable to porcelain, so the ground on which they race can make a huge impact on their performance. A horse that lifts his knees up while cantering to the start may be able to glide through mud better than a horse with a quicker movement. The state of the ground is called the 'going'. Most flat racing, as it takes place in the summer, is run on dry ground, which is described as 'good' ground. If the sun really beats down, making conditions quicker, the going may change to 'good to firm'. A lot of rain may change the going description to 'good to soft'. Wet conditions can make the ground 'soft' or 'heavy', taking the horses longer to get through it. As National Hunt is run during the winter and early spring, conditions are usually wetter, and often the going can be soft or heavy. However, the going usually changes to good by the time of the Cheltenham, Aintree, Fairyhouse and Punchestown Festivals in late spring – meaning that results of horses from the winter months cannot be taken fully at face value – as some horses like 'cut' in the ground (soft), while other horses prefer it 'like a road' (fast).

Before a horse races, the crowd can view it in the parade ring (paddock). This can lend vital clues for race-reading. These four-legged creatures cannot talk. They are not Mister Ed. So if you take a look at them, you may notice something. Is the horse relaxed with a nice even stride, or is it yanking the stablehand's arm off and exerting energy? Is the horse sweating profusely, getting worked up underneath the legs, getting on edge and threatening its chances? Does the horse's coat have a lovely glowing sheen or does it look dull? A horse's temperament cannot be underestimated, so if you can, take a look at close quarters.

Specifically in flat racing, a horse's behaviour before he or she is put into the stalls is worth watching, before you put the money down. If a horse is going mental, it may have blown its chance. If a horse is highly strung, it may not settle in the early part of the race, which means that the jockey will be pulling hard on the reins to get it relaxed while the race is ongoing – and that usually equates to wasted energy. Like all things, signs must be interpreted with a nod to the horse's previous behaviour. The 1997 Epsom Derby winner Benny The Dip sweated profusely before his races but it didn't affect his performance. In National Hunt racing, horses can often get distracted by the crowds and trainers may apply blinkers, a noseband or woolly cheekpieces to make them focus on the fence or hurdle in front of them so they don't make mistakes and lose ground to the other horses in the race. Red Rum wore a sheepskin noseband and was foot-perfect around Aintree on five occasions in the 1970s when the fences were much more daunting than they are today.

## Jockeys

When I was small I asked my Dad every day if Willie Carson had won a race. I always looked for his name in the newspaper. I liked the symmetry of the letters: W Carson. And often he would tell me that Willie Carson had won – and that made me happy. I didn't know it then, but Willie Carson won a lot of races because he was an exceptional jockey. So I was doing something as a child which we adult gamblers often forget to do. And that is to look at who is riding the horse. Tony McCoy, Ruby Walsh, Johnny Murtagh, Frankie Dettori and Kieren Fallon are all household names for a reason. You have to be a little mad to be a jockey, risking life and limb on these beasts at a top speed of 47 miles per hour.

The best jockeys can make a mockery of the handicapper's rating of a horse by giving their mount a huge advantage in a race. A jockey's skill in the saddle can be worth a number of lengths at the business end of the contest. I remember attending the 2005 Eclipse flat race at Sandown, in which the Epsom Derby winner, Motivator, ridden by Johnny Murtagh, was beaten by one of our own, Aidan O'Brien's Oratorio, a 12/1 shot ridden by Fallon. I was standing in the middle of the course on the other side of the stands beside the winning post and observed Fallon and Murtagh thundering towards me. As Fallon came closer on Oratorio, I could see him whistling at the horse. I don't know why, but it was man and horse in tandem.

On the other hand, a jockey can lose a race he should have won. In 2004, I tipped up Clan Royal in the Aintree Grand National at 10/1. The horse was ridden by Liam Cooper. I tend to become animated during the National, as it's a race I hold dear to my heart. Cooper was in an excellent position just off the leaders at half way, but the pace was furious. So, to my alarm, he hastily brought Clan Royal to the front of affairs. Down the back straight, the horse made a mistake and Cooper dropped his whip to the turf. He then proceeded to forget about The Elbow, the little kink after the last fence, and the horse lost vital ground as he veered back towards the run-in. Amberleigh House was being rousted on the outside by Graham Lee and got up to win. It was a crushing defeat. Six years later in the National, Tony McCoy would ride a textbook winning race on Don't Push It, for the same owner (JP McManus) and the same trainer (Jonjo O'Neill) of Clan Royal.

When I think of McCoy, I think of a powerful style – and an ability to get to the bottom of every horse, so no stone is left unturned. When I watch Ruby Walsh, I notice a jockey who has a superb appreciation of the pace of a race and how to conserve energy by keeping his horse in the right place at all times. Ruby also knows how to present his horses at fences, avoiding mistakes and gaining ground. In the 2000 Grand National,

Papillon and Mely Moss came to the final fence together and Walsh whipped Papillon over the fence, galvanising him to victory. Horses can be temperamental in running, so a jockey may have to switch him off at the back (a hold-up horse) or let him enjoy himself out in front (front runner).

In flat racing, pace is even more crucial, which is why Greville Starkey invited derision by leaving it too late on Dancing Brave in the 1986 Epsom Derby. On that day, Walter Swinburn on Sharastani stole a lead and never relinquished it. In the same race in 1995, Swinburn's Lammtarra looked to have much to do, but the jockey pressed the turbo button just in time for his colt to cut the field down in the last 100 yards and win. The finish is also vital on the flat, as the margins of victory and defeat are slim. Fallon is the best I have seen in a finish as he angles his body and grinds away on the horse in his own unique style. Before him, Lester Piggott was the embodiment of a jockey who knew how to ride a finish. Watch the 1977 Epsom Derby if you don't believe me.

In all sports, there are some individuals that are better than others, so it's important to see who is riding what and for whom. If Ruby Walsh or Tony McCoy are riding for a small trainer, why? He may have a good horse and want the best jockey. That's why we look at the *Racing Post* to examine strike rates. If Walsh has a 25% win rate on horses trained by Tony Martin, to an overall profit of €10 off a level €1 stake, then it must come into calculations. In 1999, Mick Fitzgerald was the then brother-in-law of trainer Paul Nicholls, and that sent off alarm bells in my head when he was booked to ride See More Business in the Cheltenham Gold Cup, rather than Double Thriller, the mount of stable jockey Joe Tizzard. Double Thriller went off a shorter price, but could only finish fourth to the winner, See More Business, who I backed at 14/1.

## Trainers

Training horses is not an easy job. It's expensive, horses can get sick, owners can lose money or decide to be fickle and not invest any more, while your competitors dominate. It's a dog eat dog business.

I have visited Aidan O'Brien's yard and seen at first hand how a magnificent trainer operates, treating the horses as individuals and using his natural talent to get the best out of them. A large and skilled stable staff, good land for the gallops, a rich benefactor and a touch of O'Brien genius makes Ballydoyle what it is.

On the jumps side, Willie Mullins has taken National Hunt training in Ireland to another level in recent years. Mullins learned the ropes from his father Paddy and was an amateur jockey. That in itself is not enough to be champion trainer. Willie Mullins has a knack of winning big races. He maximised the potential of Florida Pearl and his habit of coming home with trophies from Cheltenham attracts owners who will (in my view) play by his rules of buying decent youngsters and turning them with patience into very good jumpers.

Horses cannot be at the top of their game all year round. They have to be given a specific programme with a target in mind. When I saw Tranquil Sea easily win the 2009 Paddy Power Gold Cup in November at Cheltenham, my feeling was that he wouldn't be winning the following March at the Festival. I believed Tranquil Sea would be over the top six months later and so it proved as he couldn't repeat his November performance. Rooster Booster, the 2003 Champion Hurdle winner at Cheltenham, finished second off top weight in a big handicap one month before the 2004 Champion Hurdle, which he surprisingly lost as 11/8 favourite to the 33/1 outsider Hardy Eustace.

One thing I admired growing up about Jenny Pitman was her ability to get a horse ready for a really big day. The big day is all that matters, so when Pitman entered Royal Athlete in the 1995 Grand National, a horse which had overcome leg problems, you could safely assume Royal Athlete would put his best hooves forward. Given he went off 17/2 favourite in the 1993 Void Grand National and was a former novice chase winner at Cheltenham, Royal Athlete's 40/1 winning price was an insult. The 2010 Epsom Derby winner, Workforce, belied a statistic which said that horses beaten in the Dante Trial at York (Workforce was second) historically do not win at Epsom. Fine, but in this case the handler of Workforce was Michael Stoute, who trained what I would describe as the unexceptional Kris Kin and North Light to punch above their weight and win the Derby in the last decade. So the trainer should be factored into your selection, good or bad. Workforce broke the track record for the Derby, going back to 1780.

## Racecourses (Tracks)

I love going to the jumps festival at Leopardstown at Christmas. I have been attending since I was a teenager and it's great fun. And a big part of that is the track. Leopardstown is such a great track to watch racing. It's straightforward, left-handed (the horses race from left to right) and the fences are fair. It suits horses that like to gallop, improving as they travel through the race – and to my mind it identifies a good type of winner. There's no point in doing research on a horse race without taking course form into account. Former Cheltenham Gold Cup winner Denman ran at Punchestown in 2010 and started favourite in the betting. He proceeded to jump to the left at every fence and hated the right-handed track. When I think about Gowran Park ahead of the Thyestes Chase each year, I know that the ground is generally very testing. When I think about Naas over the jumps, I'm looking for a speedy horse as it's such a tight track. When I seek Cheltenham clues, I check out Irish horses that have run well at Navan, as Navan is a left-handed track with an uphill finish, like Cheltenham. When I look for English horses at Cheltenham, I consult Newbury form. Newbury may be a flatter course than Cheltenham, but it's left-handed and tends to attract decent runners. Although it is right-handed, Sandown also has a stiff finish, so I bear that in mind come Cheltenham time. On the flat, I check out Lingfield and Goodwood form ahead of the Epsom Derby meeting. Goodwood, unlike Epsom, is right-handed, but has similar undulations which young horses need to handle.

Obviously, if a horse takes a particular shine to a track, he may be able to surpass his form at other tracks and belittle his odds. Norton's Coin, the 100/1 winner of the 1990 Cheltenham Gold Cup, had finished second at the Festival twelve months beforehand in a race over a shorter distance. Amberleigh House was a decent if not top-level horse in Ireland before moving to Ginger McCain's yard near Liverpool. Amberleigh House became an Aintree specialist, winning the Becher Chase over the Grand National fences before winning the race itself in 2004. Desert Orchid loved right-handed courses and won the King George Chase at Kempton and the Irish Grand National at Fairyhouse. Some horses can cope with both left and right-handed courses – Sea the Stars won at Newmarket and Leopardstown in his brilliant year on the flat, while Kauto Star has adapted to Kempton and Cheltenham. The great Best Mate was more at home on left-handed tracks. He won the King George at Kempton, but it was down to sheer class rather than anything else.

## Gambling on a Nag

I have participated in one proper inside gamble on a horse, or a 'touch' as it is also called. It happened a few years ago and it came off, so I will have to create a fictitious name for the nag, lest I receive a call from the owner or trainer. Let's call the horse 'Beat The Bookies'. A friend of mine owned the horse, and he had been showing a lot on the gallops at home (the horse, not my friend). He was a stayer, a 3-mile hurdler, but he needed soft ground. My friend was decent enough to keep me in the loop. The horse's improvement at home had excited him and as the horse's previous form was over differing distances and ground, the horse had dropped to an attractive mark. In other words, he was 'well handicapped' and would have a nice racing weight. So the consensus at the yard was that this horse should win a race. A suitable race was selected. In racing speak, this would be the day when the horse would be 'off' and ready to run the race of his life. And the money would go down.

That sounds like mischievous behaviour, doesn't it? Well, we are dealing with a sport here that is based around betting and money. And the big festivals aside, it would be naïve to believe that every single horse in every single race is running to its merits. Training fees are exorbitant and 'gambles' are part of racing's charm. That's why it's so important to examine a horse's best form in race reading, because the authorities do not – and perhaps cannot – explain categorically the performance of each runner. That's also why we have a market and market movers. The horse cannot answer questions and the trainer can often squirm his way out of any stewards' inquisition. It's a fact of life, but unless a trainer blatantly uses the racecourse as a schooling ground, let's just say that, unlike football or golf, video evidence is always inconclusive.

And gambles can leave the owner and trainer with omelettes on their faces. I know of another owner who kept gambling on his horse and was dumbfounded when the horse wouldn't start winning. He would blame the track, the distance, the jockey and the ground. Eventually it dawned on everyone that the horse was 'soft', or in other words useless. The bookies know that gambles don't always come off, so they often welcome the challenge.

'Beat the Bookies' (this horse with the assumed name) was a 12/1 shot for a race on a Sunday at a well-known Irish track. The gamble was on and I was given a lot of money to place bets online for this friend. I set up over ten online betting accounts, most of them with UK-based bookmakers. The money had been deposited over the previous weeks. It was like some kind of MI5 operation, and nobody knew about it. My friend was clever enough to have the horse trained by a discreet individual. There would be no stable talk to let the cat out of the bag. At around noon, I was given the go-ahead. I had multiple windows open on Internet Explorer as I quickly tried to get the money down. I started placing as much as I was allowed to with these bookmakers, who usually allowed a €200 maximum bet. For an Irish race, a lot of them would have a maximum exposure of say €2,000 or €5,000. I managed to get on around €1,000 between 10/1 at 12/1 and then the credit-card company, out of the blue, blocked my card. Later I admired their security procedures, but at the time I went ballistic, as this friend expected the money down at the price. By the time I had screamed down the phone at the credit-card company, the price was 4/1, cut very quickly by alert bookmakers who had seen all this before. I managed to put another €500 on at 4/1. This put me quite on edge.

I was joined for the leisurely pursuit of watching the race in a Dublin turf accountant's by another friend, who wasn't exactly a racing enthusiast, but wanted to be part of the action and wagered €500 at 4/1. The race had it all. I watched quietly as 'Beat the Bookies' travelled well in behind the leaders around the first circuit. These lowly Irish races generally have no pace and don't begin in earnest until the business end. 'Beat the Bookies' was still going well four hurdles out before coming under pressure. He had a very good jockey on board, which lowered my internal combustion. The problem was that we hadn't gone each way, and another horse began to stretch clear. This was meant to have been a walk in the park. *No*, I thought, but the words wouldn't come out. The leader was looking like the winner before falling at the final flight. It was an incredible development. His mishap left 'Beat the Bookies' and a third horse to battle it out up the run-in. We still hadn't gone each way. This was meant to be a perfect gamble, an easy touch. "*Come on!*" shouted my friend in the shop out of the blue. His urging at the screens uncoiled my emotions, as I then began to shout, effing and blinding. The horses were bobbing away like swimmers and I was clenching my teeth, screaming among the customers on this sleepy Sunday. My hands were outstretched, the veins on my neck pumping and face gurning. 'Beat the Bookies' got up in the last few strides to literally win on the line. *"Yeeeaaasss!"* I screamed, high-fiving my friend, stomping around like it was my own living room. The other gents in the shop knew what was going on, but I'm sure they were wondering how much we had won. My feelings were a mixture of utter exhilaration and sheer relief. We collected our winnings and promptly left. I rang my friend to congratulate him. It was a good coup.

Coups are very rare and I doubt I'll see another one. Hard work is 99% of sports betting.

In general, the usefulness of inside information is entirely dependent on the source of the information and their record of giving you good information in the past. It's best to stick to your own opinion and treat the majority of 'tips' with a pinch of salt unless the source is rock solid. When people ask me for a tip, my opinion is completely based on research and interpretation. In horse-racing, I find market moves are a much better guide than whispers. At a big meeting like Cheltenham, inside information has its limits due to the competitiveness of the racing. The average winner at Cheltenham in 2010 was nearly 14/1, so unless you have the trainer, the owner, the jockey, or the manager at the other end of a line, follow your own path in the battle with the bookies. Don't be swayed.

Coping with an agonising loss when you see a really good bet and it doesn't come off is important to being a successful punter, because it happens all the time. To give one example, there was a horse called Merchant's Friend, who was trained in Ireland by Tom Taaffe before moving to Charlie Mann in England. His performances improved on the 'mainland' and caught my eye. I have a cousin, who lives in Watford, called Sohan. The great Sohan is also a punter – more of a poker fiend – and he and I compare notes on occasion. We were talking about the jumps when I started blabbering on about Merchant's Friend. The horse had progressed under Mann to finish fifth in the Hennessy Gold Cup, the big handicap chase at Newbury in November. It's a race that has often thrown up Grand National winners. With Merchant's Friend's best form in my brain, I backed him each way in the Kim Muir Chase at the 2004 Cheltenham Festival. At 33/1. The horse was sent out in front and when they went out into the country he began to forge well ahead. It was looking good. In fact, coming down the hill, there was Merchant's Friend, and nothing else. I was glowing with excitement. My faith in this animal was about to be rewarded. At the final fence, he was 20 lengths clear, with only Cheltenham's mountainous hill to conquer. Merchant's Friend became Merchant's Enemy as his energy emptied up the straight. He was getting very tired, and another horse, Maximise, was flying. I wanted to run onto the track and whip my horse, and then his jockey. Maximise got up to win on the line. A complete sense of deflation overcame me. I felt like the Hindenburg, if one can. Maximise had won at 40/1.

I rang Sohan.

"Did you see that?" I asked, gutted.

"Yeah," came the Cockney reply. He started laughing. "I backed Maximise!"

You need to take the punches on the chin, or you won't spot the next Merchant's Friend. The one that wins.

# Chapter 6

*On The Driving Range*

I don't play golf. I find attempting to do so a complete waste of time. I wasn't born with hand to eye co-ordination or eye to hand co-ordination and, if I was, I must have lost it on the way out of Holles Street (where babies are born in Dublin). I have tried it and I am useless. I get blisters on the driving range and the ball doesn't go far when I hit it. I can't figure out the greens. I have chronic hayfever problems. I don't believe in getting frustrated at something I am not good at, so I don't partake in spoiling a good walk, or what they call pitch and putt. I settle for the PlayStation and shoot low scores on that in the comfort of my living room.

However, here's how it is, folks. I'm serious about watching golf. I know what the words birdie, bogey, par and eagle mean, and if you don't, you need to take a trip to the Glossary. I'm addicted to watching this gentlemanly pursuit (which is becoming more popular with the ladies).

I believe it's where most of the money is in sports betting. It's much more fun for me to relax at home and have a beverage and watch my investments. You can also make golf betting work for you and I'm going to tell you how.

There are two big professional tours in golf, the US Tour and the European Tour. Both tours sanction 4 'Major' Championships, upon which golfing greatness is measured. They are the US Masters, held in Augusta, Georgia, in April; the US Open, held at a rota of courses around the United States in June; the Open, otherwise known as the British Open, which is held in England or Scotland in July; and the US PGA Championship, staged once again at a rota of courses around the United States in August. Most courses in the USA are parkland courses, beautifully designed, lush, and geared towards 'target golf' where the player knows exactly what needs to be done from tee to cup. The ball in the USA tends to be played a lot more in the air, unlike in the Open. The Open Championship, which is the oldest major, is played on links courses i.e. courses on land adjoining the sea. Links courses require a greater variety of shots and their defence against low scores is the wind from the sea, demanding more imagination from players who need to bump and run shots up to the flag and extract themselves from bunkers which are much more severe than in America. An example of a parkland course in Ireland is Mount Juliet. Ballybunion, on the other hand, is a links course.

Back in 2003 – with Steve Flesch having changed my wardrobe but not my life – I really believed I was Midas. One week later David Toms was loitering around the shop window at the Wachovia Championship, so I waded in at 9/1. Result. Toms won it easily. I was winning a lot of money and felt really 'in the zone' as gamblers sometimes do. You can acquire an unusual clarity. I have been there. So much so that as I began my analysis for the US Open in June, it was all about one player, Jim Furyk. The American with the loopy swing was playing the best golf of his career, with ten Top 10 finishes in fourteen starts, entering proceedings at that year's host course, Olympia Fields. He was Double Carpet (33/1) and the narrow 18 holes in Illinois suited his game perfectly. He had contended (i.e. was close to winning) in the US Open before, in 1996 and 1997, so he knew the script. Furyk is a boringly effective player, a player who hits fairways and greens through the eye of a needle. He doesn't smash the ball 350 yards, but he's an excellent lag putter, which means that he usually makes par (the required number of shots on a hole from which a score is measured – i.e. 1 under par or 1 over par) by finding the cup on the green in two putts. Of course Furyk won, and two months into my tipping career on radio he had placed a feather in my cap. I had examined his statistics, his recent form, age, his readiness for a major and his past experience in whittling down all of the potential choices. A 33/1 winner that could be backed. A 33/1 winner in horse-racing is a lot harder to find. A 33/1 winner doesn't exist in most other sports.

Jim Furyk at 33/1. Padraig Harrington at 22/1. Stephen Ames at 40/1. Geoff Ogilvy at 40/1. Bo Van Pelt at 50/1. These are some of the golf winners which I have tipped on the radio over the years. Considering there are 45 Official US PGA Tour events in the calendar year (including the Majors), if you have a winner and maybe have a couple of each-way golfers placed at big odds and if you have some other sporting winners in the year, you are looking at a profit. All of this is dependent on keeping your stakes sensible and consistent, but I made an error on air in 2010. I expected to strike it lucky early on and I recommended placing excessive stakes on certain golfers in certain tournaments who didn't perform. Or didn't perform at the right time.

Nothing went right for me over the airwaves in 2010 and that's why I was issuing profit warnings. Let me see how the stars didn't align. I tipped Jeff Overton each-way in a tournament in January. He didn't contend – and then went on to finish in the Top 5 on five occasions. I tipped Jason Day in February and he then went and won in May at 150/1. The trend continued. I tipped Rory McIlroy in March and he won a month later at 66/1. I tipped Justin Rose in March and he subsequently won twice. I tipped Dustin Johnson and Paul Casey at the Masters in April – Johnson was in contention at both the US Open in June and US PGA in August, Casey at the British Open in July. I tipped Rickie Fowler and Ricky Barnes in May and a fortnight later they were both placed at the Memorial Tournament. I tipped Martin Kaymer in the US Open and he won the next US major – the US PGA.

This gets worse. I personally backed but did not tip three winners: Anthony Kim in Houston at 25/1; Zach

Johnson in the Colonial Tournament at 54/1; and then Rose in the Memorial one week later at 84/1. Sorry – it's not a sob story – but I just wanted to illustrate how important it is to keep the faith in golf betting.

It would bore the listeners for me to tip golfers every week. That's not what the slot is about – but I do back them and I've even set up a Twitter account to share my thoughts.

Golf is clean – clean as a whistle and anally so, if you saw the ruling which effectively disqualified Dustin Johnson from having a chance to win the 2010 US PGA Championship. Johnson was penalised two strokes for placing his club on the ground before taking a bunker shot on the 72nd hole, which you are not supposed to do. The course, Whistling Straits, was very sandy, and every piece of sand was classified as a bunker, despite there being no distinction between traditional bunkers and trampled down waste areas.

Anyway, I digress. Golf is all about honour. To call a golfer a cheat is the worst thing you could do – the game is sacred – and with television cameras recording every move there is no hiding place. So we know now that the only impediments to success are the golfer and his competitors – not a horse who cannot tell you how he is feeling or an owner who doesn't want his horse to win because he is waiting for a big gamble. Team sports have increased variables, which despite fewer outcomes actually increases the risk in my view, as the odds are so marginal. Golf is about Mr Harrington on a given week versus 150 others. And the number of golfers in the tournament creates a decent book for you to gain a potentially significant return from a relatively small risk. Golf prices are big because of the number of players in a tournament. So if Chelsea are 1/1, or even money to beat Liverpool at Anfield, you will win €2,000 if you stake €2,000. On the other hand, if Justin Rose is 84/1 to win the 2010 Memorial Tournament on Betfair, which he was, his victory returned €2,000 (net commission of 5%) for an outlay of just €25. Of course Chelsea have a far better chance from a probability standpoint, but the financial risk is lower with golf. It's important to forget about the number of players – stick to three each-way selections when you bet on a tournament – and treat it as a long-term project. Golf betting is fun because you can back a player (i.e. Justin Rose) and then watch the tournament for four days. If he plays well and becomes a contender, you really get a run for your money and it's a valuable experience. It is also educational as you are gaining knowledge all the time by sitting on your sofa watching other players. It's the Discovery Channel for bettors.

Watching golf is the first piece of advice I would give. Golf is such a psychological game for the player that to examine their mistakes when the pressure is on, especially on the final day of a tournament, is illuminating. A player may take the lead and a smooth game then comes under pressure. They start thinking about the victory and suddenly they lose composure and the shot is in the rough or the water. On the other hand, the player may have nerves of steel and you know he is going to finish the job. Once Padraig Harrington won his first US PGA Tour event, it was easier for him to do it again. Once he won his first major championship, he knew the rituals. It's the only sport I know where players employ individual psychologists to remove the clutter from their head space. Sergio Garcia and Adam Scott have been very talented players over the last decade, but neither has won a major. Darren Clarke is an exceptionally gifted golfer but he has no majors and fellow Paddy Harrington has three. Greg Norman never won a major in America. Colin Montgomerie, a winner of the European Tour money list seven times in succession, has never won a major – period. So keeping an eye on a player's 'bottle' or nerve is a key factor when that hand hovers over the computer or the phone.

Of course natural talent has everything to do with everything. That's why Jack Nicklaus won eighteen majors and Tiger Woods is the greatest player in history. If a player has no mental barriers, he can be very successful if he possesses God-given talent. That's how Woods became so dominant so early – he won the US Open by 15 shots at Pebble Beach in 2000 because he was better than everyone else to start, he was mentally calm and he was playing his best golf that week.

Your judgement of a golfer's nerve is something you need to assimilate by watching. However, there are two clear factors which historical analysis on paper will show are crucial to selecting contenders. They are: a) course form, and b) recent form. Every golfer is different – and some have very different skills. Dustin Johnson, the

American, hits the ball like a missile off the tee, but that doesn't mean he is always accurate. Heath Slocum, another American, hits the ball like an arrow off the tee but isn't as precise with his irons. Padraig Harrington is a magician in getting the ball down in par from off the green, but why is he in trouble in the first place? Robert Allenby of Australia is a brilliant ball striker but an average putter. American Brad Faxon was a brilliant putter but an average ball striker. Rory McIlroy has everything, but his putting can be inconsistent and he remains inexperienced when it comes to course management. Jack Nicklaus was the doyen of course management.

The course can determine a lot. Some players fade the ball (which means they shape it from left to right) and some draw the ball (which means they shape it from right to left) depending on their swing. Some players hit it low, which helps in the wind, as the flight of the ball is not affected as much, while others balloon it and land it softly. Phil Mickelson has never contended at the Open in Britain due to a high ball-flight which is unsuited to the wind and his inability to read the greens as well as he does in the USA. If you lay Phil at the Open every year, you will always win.

All of these issues must be noted when we see where the tournament is to be played. Does the player like the course or is he seeing it for the first time that week? You know yourself, if you play the same course every week and, unlike me, have some talent for hitting the ball more than 10 yards, then surely you will get better as you become more comfortable and familiar. Bo Van

Pelt, the 50/1 winner I tipped in Milwaukee in 2009, had played well at the Brown Deer Park course before, so he was carrying good memories into that event. I noted that when he was really struggling a few years ago, Van Pelt shot three good rounds in Milwaukee. And if a course suits a player's eye, they generally perform to a certain level. That level will be good if they are in decent form, which brings us to the second factor, recent form. Unless he is Tiger Woods, a player cannot keep churning out incredible results week by week for ten months. A player may ride a hot streak and win a couple of tournaments, but they are not machines. Their driving off the tee may be wayward one week, or they may have problems with the putter which holds them back. Or off-course issues which hamper their concentration. So I often look to players who have been playing nicely and are ready to peak, rather than a player who was brilliant in March, but who has lost his mojo by August. Generally, as my analysis will show, if a player is feeling good about his game, it is easier for him to carry solid form into subsequent events, allowing you the opportunity to capitalise in the betting market.

The caveat is that in this very mental game a player may discover a little bit of magic which can result in an incredible week. In July 2009, Stewart Cink won the (British) Open at Turnberry at 175/1. He had played alongside eventual winner Padraig Harrington in 2007 in the final group at Carnoustie, finishing sixth. The Georgian (America, not Eastern Bloc) toured County

Clare before going to Turnberry, drinking Guinness and playing Lahinch to familiarise himself again with the conditions he would face in Scotland. Cink was under the radar. During a quiet year he had finished twenty-seventh at the US Open, but reached the Top 10 in the Memorial Tournament one month before the British Open. So he was lukewarm, but he hadn't caught fire. However, this was a top player, with a Ryder Cup CV, a near miss in the 2001 US Open and five tour wins to boot. So the fact he found some magic at Turnberry is a lesson that recent form isn't a panacea. It's just a tool for your armoury, as we are not dealing with an exact science.

I concentrate my betting on the US PGA Tour for reasons which I will explain later. When I research a tournament on a Tuesday, perhaps for a Thursday bet, I use the PGA Tour website and other sources to consult course form, recent form, win ratios and various other statistics. I want to know statistics on Driving Distance (how far the ball is hit by a player off the tee); Driving Accuracy (the ability of the player to find the fairway and avoid the rough); Total Driving (distance and accuracy combined); Greens in Regulation (the amount of greens a player hits with a tee shot on a par 3, a second shot on a par 4, and a third shot on a par 5); Ball Striking (total driving and greens in regulation combined); Putts Per Green in Regulation (how many putts a player takes for every green hit); Scrambling (when a player successfully saves par after missing a green); Sand Saves (how many times a player saves par from a bunker); Putts Per Round (total putts for 18 holes); Birdie Average (average number of birdies per round played) and Scoring Average (average score for the year). There are more statistics which can aid your thought process, but these are the main areas which I rely upon when trying to solve the weekly jigsaw puzzle. Note, and this is very important, that I want to have an overall view of a player's history of winning tournaments, even at a lower level. If players win in college, or on the secondary tours, then when they graduate to the US Tour or European Tour, I want to be on their side. Winning is winning, and it doesn't matter at which level it is at. A player that knows how to win can often repeat the process quicker than somebody who is more consistent but lacks a killer instinct.

The remaining chapters on golf in this book are divided into two. The first will deal with the 4 Major Championships and the second will consist of a guide to the US PGA Tour as currently constructed, examining the 2010 results, before a brief synopsis of the European Tour.

# Part 2

*Sports and Events*

# Chapter 7

## Cheltenham

Now I don't know if the horse Frenchman's Creek was named after the Daphne Du Maurier novel, nor do I really care. However, I received quite a magical gift on my first ever day at the Cheltenham Festival in March 2002 when, wandering around in the bookies' ring after watching two of my tips come in, I noticed a £20 win docket for Frenchman's Creek lying on the ground. The horse had won the 3-mile handicap chase around half an hour earlier. Luckily I'm the kind of guy who slouches about. I'm not a moper, it's just poor physical posture on my part. Anyway, my 'moping' allowed me to notice this docket. I looked around, startled. If you know who Charlie Bucket is, you can imagine how I felt. There was nobody around me in search of a losing docket and nobody in close proximity ready to shout "Thief!" and report me to the nearest constabulary. So I carefully picked up the docket and walked coolly to the bookmaker who had issued it. He in turn handed me £180, as Frenchman's Creek was an 8/1 winner. I sauntered away, my heart pumping. I then placed £40 on The Bushkeeper, who won the next race at 9/2. I think the Gods were giving me some kind of special welcome. A complimentary drink on the house as it were. I've always had a pull towards Cheltenham, because I know from experience that what it giveth, it can taketh away. And that's the charm.

Cheltenham. The word conjures many images in my mind, but it's the goosebumps I feel every year that I never grow tired of. The first day of Cheltenham is Christmas Day for National Hunt racing fans and, in recent years, the hype has increased in the preceding weeks, with preview nights and publications to send us in the direction of the certainties. The meeting was extended from three days to four in 2005. I always tell people that once you go to Cheltenham, you never want to miss it again. Cheltenham has a very Irish flavour, despite its location in the Cotswolds in the county of Gloucestershire in the South West of England. It is what they say it is – a pilgrimage. We take over the place for the week, despite being outnumbered by the locals. And back home, Cheltenham week engages the masses – those of us who take a half-day to place bets and watch the racing at home or with friends in the local pubs beside the adjoining bookies. That the meeting often coincides with St Patrick's Day adds to the appeal. For Irish people, this week is a celebration of sporting pride – pride in the fact that we can go and compete in the 'Olympics' of the jumps game and win, ever since the late 1940s when Vincent O'Brien shocked the English racing establishment by flying over horses to win Gold Cups and Champion Hurdles with a mould-breaking regularity.

So what is it? The course has a lot to do with it. It's a theatre. The imposing Cleeve Hill overlooks the racecourse and at the other side is a towering grandstand. The track is undulating, so like Epsom it has the ability to provide the stiffest test, as the horses go uphill and out into the country, downhill at speed and then up a punishing climb to the finish line. The meeting attracts the best horses, the best jockeys and the best trainers in National Hunt. The races are run at a frenetic pace, much more so than ordinary meetings. Every horse is trying, and in a sport that attracts its fair share of skulduggery and suspicion, its competitiveness is crucial for its appeal. Every jumps owner dreams of a winner at Cheltenham. And it's war inside the betting ring and the shops too. There are now twenty-seven races at the Festival, spanning four days, and a profitable Tuesday can quickly turn into a disastrous week for either a backer or a layer by the middle of the Thursday. With 50,000 people on course each day for four days, Cheltenham is relentless. The races hit you like punches, and once you have dusted yourself down, another punch is on the way.

I've done well at Cheltenham, making a profit on my charity bets for the *Breakfast Show* over the week seven years out of nine since 2002. Unfortunately, 2010 wasn't one of those years! The reason I like Cheltenham is that if you do your research, you can identify likely candidates for the winner's enclosure, as many factors repeat themselves in guiding you to the correct horse. Due to public interest, the bookmakers must be competitive against each other, so there is great value to be had in terms of price and each-way offers. One big winner can make for a successful punting week.

In terms of preparation, the best thing to do to enhance your chances of winning money is to watch as much racing as possible. That goes for every sport of course – reading a race review or a report is no substitute for the real thing. Thus, if you fancy taking a purist's view, it's important to watch the big races from November onwards and if you are serious, to subscribe to the racing channels, *At the Races* and *Racing UK*. Watching races will make you connect the dots by remembering horses in the future when you study a race card. It's good policy to watch archived races online, especially the previous year's Festival, to get a feel for the type of horse required to win at the track. It's also advisable to look at any trials at the track from November onwards.

I keep mentioning the course because Cheltenham really is unique and you need a horse suited to a left-handed track which can handle the undulations. Ascot and Kempton are right-handed tracks that often suit speedy types, and form at these places doesn't always equate for Cheltenham. Many horses having a marked preference for travelling either left or right-handed, Cheltenham houses repeat offenders in that horses that like the place often come back and win. There are two tracks at Cheltenham. The Old Course used to have a tricky downhill fence and a shorter finish, but has been altered to mirror the New Course, with two fences in a longer straight. As regards ground conditions, racing in winter tends to be on soft or heavy ground, which can make races a real stamina test. There are horses which love it, but other horses hate it, so you must identify the optimum conditions for your fancy, especially as the ground at Cheltenham is usually on the good side.

Another key component of race-reading is the best form for a horse. Recent form is important and many races at Cheltenham are won by horses which won last time out, but it's foolhardy to discard a horse's best form, especially in handicaps, as trainers often plot a horse for a big race at the Festival by keeping a little in reserve. So if you tend to back horses every week, I would recommend a subscription to the *Racing Post* website. The industry standard allows you to analyse the lifetime performance of your horse, rather than sifting through the paper on race day and only analysing the most recent form of the horse you have picked out. The best example I can give of this is Fota Island, who I tipped in the 2005 Grand Annual Handicap Chase off a featherweight. This Irish horse had finished sixth in a Champion Hurdle and was underrated with only 10 stone on his back. None of the English tipsters picked him out and he won at 7/1.

The form of a trainer is noteworthy, especially if a trainer has a poor record at the Festival (Noel Meade), has had a poor season (Alan King in 2009-10), or on the other hand, always tends to strike gold at the sport's biggest meeting (in recent times Paul Nicholls, Nicky Henderson, and Willie Mullins). There is a reason why Ruby Walsh has been lord of the manor at Cheltenham in recent years, while Tony McCoy has not. Not only is it down to Ruby's prowess in the saddle, it's because he is riding for the champion trainers in Ireland and England, Willie Mullins and Paul Nicholls respectively.

I have mixed views on preview nights, because you can find yourself the victim of information overload. Remember this is Cheltenham, and everybody wants to win. If you go to a preview night, it's sometimes better to attend the low-key events, where guests are more forthright with their views. Your own view can be as valid as the next person's.

In terms of betting it's often good to focus on one horse for the week or one per day and go for it, keeping the rest of your investments small. With big fields and bookmakers eager to entice new customers, you must go each way and take the value on offer (1/4 the odds, the first five places in some races). In 2009 I tipped up Dunguib for the Champion Bumper on the morning of the race at 7/1 on the basis of what I saw in his races and some very good information I received that the trainer, Philip Fenton, felt it was the best bumper horse he had ever come into contact with. Knowing that Philip Fenton was the best amateur jockey for years and rode thousands of bumper horses, that information was good enough for me. So I chose him as my horse for the week and bet accordingly. Luckily, Dunguib turned into an aeroplane from the top of the hill and left the rest for dead. It is some feeling when you back a Cheltenham winner at decent odds. Sohan from Watford rang me and told me he was shaking. He was on Dunguib too.

What not to do if you are having a bad week is chase your losses. You must remind yourself that you could lose for three days running and win it all back and more on the Friday. Don't dig a hole for yourself in the meantime.

Sometimes I go to Cheltenham and I feel like I have given myself a lobotomy and stuffed pages of the *Racing Post* into my head. I have seen every race and every piece of information has been processed. And then I start tipping and it's a total disaster. I did this in 2006 and again in 2010. When I realised that 2010 was going to be a losing week for me, I was resigned to my fate. I wasn't happy about it, but I knew I was a little out of step in terms of my tipping and it wasn't going to get any better. I had to rely on laying to come out ahead personally.

As I am so well prepared, I often select the most rational winner in my mind and then create ten reasons for why it won't win. And then the horse gives two hooves to my devil's advocacy by winning, as if to say 'Neigh Neigh Neigh Neigh Neigh!', flashing his rear end in my face. Other times I tell Ian Dempsey that I have come across a stone-cold certainty, having whipped myself into a frenzy of devout belief the night before. I have in the past exclaimed, "Get €200 of our charity bank on it now. *Now!*" It must be the early morning starts. I did this when Well Chief was running in the

2007 Queen Mother Champion Chase. He fell at the second fence. My face went as white as a sheet. There really is no such thing as a certainty in racing. We learn this often. And if we don't learn it, the gods put in a call to headquarters to ensure we are told again and again.

On the other hand, when you are relaxed and can see things clearly, sometimes you just can't stop winning. Even at Cheltenham. Unfortunately I don't know the secret as to why this is the case, apart from knowledge, confidence and the ability not to clutter your mind. In 2005, I put £10 each way on Arcalis in the first race, the Supreme Novices' Hurdle, at 25/1 on the Tote. The bet was placed on the basis of the horse's decent flat form and the fact that he was running on his favoured quick ground, as opposed to the quagmires which were commonplace that winter. Boom! Arcalis wins. The next day I placed £20 each way on Idole First in the Coral Cup at 45/1. Again on the Tote. Boom! Idole First wins. The wins can give you belief and the ammunition in your pocket. When this happens, when you are on a roll, keep going, as long as you maintain your stakes at a sensible level. What you must not do is start calling it 'the bookie's money'. 'The bookie's money' is what some punters label money that they didn't have before, but now possess after winning it. If it is 'the bookie's money' it increases your possibility of losing it, because the psychological hit won't be as bad if you don't think it is your money. You need to forget all that fishwife claptrap and remember that any money won is now your money.

Now not all of us have the time to watch racing on a regular basis or subscribe to specialist Racing TV channels. So I will give you a brief guide to Cheltenham. There are four big races: the Champion Hurdle over 2 miles on the Tuesday; the Champion Chase over 2 miles on the Wednesday; the World Hurdle over 3 miles on the Thursday; and the Gold Cup steeplechase over 3¼ miles on the Friday. The big four races are Grade 1 Championship events, so in each of the four every horse carries the same amount of weight as its rivals. There are also supplementary races which contain strong trends which I will touch upon to help you negotiate your journey through this March madness.

The 2010 **Champion Hurdle** was won by **Binocular at 9/1**. This horse beat Khyber Kim into second place, with Zaynar in third. Why? Could we have backed the nag? Yes, we could have. I tipped Khyber Kim because I felt he had electric speed, went well fresh (was able to perform without a recent run) and possessed course form, with two wins at the track in November and December of 2009. He justified my faith in him, but found one too good.

Binocular was a real hindsight winner, and the sight of Tony McCoy cruising round with plenty in hand, jumping superbly and coasting clear caused many people to hold their heads and utter expletives. Binocular was second as a four-year-old in the Supreme Novices' Hurdle over the same trip of 2 miles at the 2008 Festival, before finishing half a length third in the Champion Hurdle in

2009 after starting in the betting as the 6/4 favourite. There were doubts over his ability to get up the hill at Cheltenham in 2009, but watching the running of the race, he actually got outpaced before staying on strongly. Taking another look at past races is vital. McCoy had suffered an injury before that race in 2009, which may have affected his strength in the finish, but the main reason I can pinpoint for Binocular's improved and winning display in 2010 is age.

From 1985 until 2008, no five-year-old won the Champion Hurdle. A horse called Katchit broke that trend in 2008, but that was a really weak renewal (i.e. version of the race in comparison to other years) of the race. The key here is that horses need to fill out in their frame and physically improve. Age is a big factor in this regard, especially as the lifetime of a National Hunt racehorse is short. And in a Champion Hurdle, a horse needs to have the requisite blend of speed and stamina to win. Binocular disappointed in two starts at the back end of 2009, but his trainer Nicky Henderson kept working on him, the old sparkle returned, and the horse began to give McCoy a good feeling again in the week leading up to the race. Henderson had ruled Binocular out of the 2010 Champion Hurdle in February with a muscle injury, but the same thing had happened with Kicking King in the 2005 Cheltenham Gold Cup and he went on to win. If a horse lines up for a big race on the day, you can take it that connections believe it will do itself justice. So the lesson from Binocular is that his class shone through in the end and one must look towards the class acts in level weights races.

My record in the Champion Hurdle has been pretty bare. I tipped Hors La Loi III to win at 10/1 in 2002, which he did, and I have been tilting at windmills since. Hors La Loi had the benefit of proven course form after finishing second to Istabraq in the Champion Hurdle in 2000 and winning the Supreme Novices' Hurdle in 1999.

I have had to adjust my thinking in recent years due to Cheltenham's watering policy, whereby they artificially water the course the week before the Festival to prevent horses getting injured if it is dry in the preceding weeks and the ground gets too fast. It's led to a situation where former flat horses like Istabraq have been joined in the list of winners for the Champion Hurdle in the past decade by the more traditionally bred National Hunt staying types such as Hardy Eustace and Brave Inca. The Champion Hurdle is the fourth race of the Festival, so watering has more of an impact then than on races run on the Friday as watering cannot take place during racing. The Irish record in the race has been respectable in modern times. Irish horses went empty-handed for fourteen years between Dawn Run (1984) and Istabraq (1998). We won the race four times in a row (2004 to 2007) but the locals have been in the ascendancy since then.

In terms of research, the previous year's race is a starting point, followed by the Punchestown Champion Hurdle in April, the Bula Hurdle at Cheltenham in December, the Leopardstown Christmas Hurdle, the Irish Champion Hurdle at Leopardstown in January and the Kingwell Hurdle at Wincanton in February.

Two other things to note about the Champion Hurdle. There have only been three winners older than eight in the last sixty years and it's been forty years since a winner of the previous year's Supreme Novices' Hurdle has followed up twelve months later by winning the race.

The **Champion Chase** went to Ireland in 2010, as **Big Zeb**, a **10/1** shot, won for Wexford trainer Colm Murphy, from Forpadydeplasterer in second and Kalahari King back in third. I had one strong opinion in this race and that was that Master Minded, the odds-on favourite, would not win. I have already had my rant about laying and I hope it will seep into tipping sooner rather than later. I was against Master Minded, as although he had won the previous two renewals of the race, he had fractured a rib earlier in the season and the horse he defeated on his return from that injury, Mahogany Blaze, was no Champion Chase contender. Visually, to me, I wasn't sure that Master Minded was the same horse and with the ground drying all the time, he had to be taken on at 4/5.

To me, Big Zeb was a shock winner. As we say in racing: "I couldn't have him!" This horse nearly beat Master Minded at Punchestown in 2009 and he had the gears, but his jumping was clumsy. He had fallen four times in his career, a record which included a horrendous fall in the Champion Chase of 2009. His only other excursion across the Irish Sea resulted in a 33-length defeat at Sandown in December 2009, so I would also have put him down as a dodgy traveller. Horses like a routine and not all of them appreciate boat trips or plane rides like the rest of us. However, Murphy, a former protégé of Aidan O'Brien, knows more about horses than I will ever care to remember and he had his star spot on when it mattered. Drying ground was a major help in his success and another key was a brilliant positive ride by jockey Barry Geraghty, who let the horse enjoy himself. Murphy felt that giving Big Zeb a two-month break until Cheltenham worked wonders – and the team obviously found a way to harness the animal's speed over the stiff Prestbury Park fences (Prestbury Park is another name for Cheltenham – think City of Manchester Stadium and Eastlands).

Historically, the Champion Chase has been a straightforward race to predict, as the fields can be quite small and it really becomes a race for 2-mile specialists. There is no room for jumping errors at such a pace, which is why I was put off Big Zeb. I tipped Flagship Uberalles in 2002, off the back of his win in the novice race, the Arkle Chase in 1999 and the fact that the ground was too fast when he disappointed in the Champion Chase in 2000. Moscow Flyer in 2003 and Azertyuiop in 2004 were well fancied given their Arkle Chase wins as novices and their form around the time of their victories, but Master Minded's wide margin success in 2008 was a shock as he was a five-year-old and horses of that age just did not win the Queen Mother. Anyway, he turned out to be freakishly good. The only big surprise of recent times was 16/1 chance Newmill in 2006, but that was on lightning quick ground and he did have strong hurdling form. In terms of age, there's only been one winner at ten years of age or older since 1997 and that was the great Moscow Flyer. Half of the last eight winners have been Irish-trained. The Tingle Creek Chase at Sandown in December is a class race in itself and the leading trial. You need a good 'un in the race – Master Minded is the only recent winner who didn't have a Grade 1 Chase success.

Other races to note for research are the Victor Chandler Chase at Ascot in January and the Game Spirit Chase at Newbury in February. Also, unlike the Supreme Novices' Hurdle, note the previous year's Arkle Chase result over the same distance, as the last twelve Arkle winners to race the following season finished in the first three.

The 2010 **World Hurdle** was a procession for **5/6** favourite **Big Buck's**. It turned out to be a steering job for jockey Ruby Walsh. One could not have put the mortgage on the horse, especially as his trainer Paul Nicholls had an odds-on chance beaten in the Champion Chase. Nevertheless, Big Buck's was the type of horse to get better with age and, as a seven-year-old, his performance level increased dramatically from his win in the 2009 race to 2010. Normally Big Buck's is a lazy horse who unleashes a devastating boost of acceleration to win his races, but this time Walsh didn't need to move a muscle, as his mount bounded up the hill without the jockey having to look for his whip. The big lesson about this horse is that he was once touted as a Gold Cup chaser, but couldn't handle fences, so they reverted back to the smaller obstacles over 3 miles. In racing language, gears are gears, and like Champion Chaser Newmill, if a horse can adjust from hurdles to fences, or vice versa, then there's nothing to stop them becoming a champion in a different sphere. Now the World Hurdle isn't a handicap, but you should always watch horses in a big race that have a lower rating from the official handicapper over either hurdles or fences, because a trainer may deliberately seek a winning advantage by changing the horse's discipline. Top hurdle horse Grimes won the Galway Plate over fences in 2001 in this way.

For the World Hurdle, you need to forget about five-year-olds, because no five-year-old has ever won the race. I blame the distance of 3 miles, which is just too much for a horse of that age in a top race. It's been a quiet race for Irish-trained horses – Dorans Pride was our last winner in 1995. Also, keep an eye out for horses bred in France, as French-breds have won five of the last nine runnings. In terms of trials, the Cleeve Hurdle over the course and distance in January is the starting point. The next best trial is the Long Walk Hurdle at Ascot in December.

The horse I put up on the radio in the 2010 World Hurdle and one of my only success stories in a terrible punting week was Time For Rupert at 20/1, who finished a clear second. I liked the way this horse ran in lesser races, winning handicaps at Aintree and Cheltenham by showing a gutsy attitude and I felt he could step up even further. He did that by finishing second in a recognised trial at the course, so he ticked the boxes to contend: course form; confirmation that he would stay the distance; and a rapid rate of improvement. Now, I wish I had done the same in selecting a horse for the Gold Cup.

The 2010 **Cheltenham Gold Cup** was won by **Imperial Commander** at **7/1**. This tough chaser spoilt all the hype and marketing that centred on a duel between Kauto Star and Denman by taking their measure in imperious fashion. Imperial Commander, like many chasing stars, began life as a winning point-to-point horse in Ireland, before joining the yard of Gloucestershire trainer Nigel Twiston Davies, who lives just down the road from the racecourse. Handy for celebrating. Imperial Commander was made to race at Cheltenham, as he jumps and gallops for ever and he is a course specialist. Going into the Gold Cup, Imperial Commander had five Cheltenham wins from nine course starts under his saddle. It was one of the reasons I tipped him to win the Ryanair Chase over 2½ miles in 2009 at 13/2. However, I was sceptical about Imperial Commander at the Gold Cup trip, as horses need to tackle 3¼ miles against the very best, and Kauto Star and Denman had proven themselves to be the very best.

It was impossible to lay odds-on shot Kauto Star, as he had won the 2007 and 2009 stagings of the Gold Cup and the King George Chase at Kempton at Christmas for the fourth successive time by a distance. He was coming into the race in the best form of his life, but I did have nagging doubts. For some reason, I have never liked the speedy Kauto Star, probably because he is not the most natural jumper of a fence I have seen. For a horse to be classified as a true steeplechasing legend in my eyes, I want to see inch-perfect jumping, which Best Mate produced on the way to his hat-trick of Gold Cup wins. Kauto Star fell in the 2006 Champion Chase at Cheltenham and in the 2008 Gold Cup, I was utterly convinced that the Paul Nicholls stablemate Denman would usurp Kauto Star, so I confidently tipped him at 2/1. I love Denman. They nickname him 'The Tank' – but all I hear is a chainsaw sound in my head when he runs. He is a real tough old-fashioned chaser, a magnificent jumper and a relentless galloper. He galloped Kauto Star into the ground that day, but I believe the sticky ground hindered Kauto Star's jumping. With rain falling, the ground for the 2010 Gold Cup was once again sticky, which planted further doubts about Kauto Star in my mind. That's why it's judicious to hold your powder dry for as long as possible before a race, to see the ground conditions and the way the market is moving. I could not be having Denman though. Diagnosed with a heart condition after the 2008 win, he didn't run to the same level until the 2009 Hennessy and I felt, at ten years of age, these massive performances were taking too much out of him. So I chose Cooldine, the winner of the 3-mile RSA Novices' Chase at the 2009 Festival and saddled by Ireland's champion trainer, Willie Mullins. I was counting on Cooldine to show the same level of form that he did in trouncing the field in that novice race, but it was Imperial Commander, and not Cooldine, who grew wings over the gruelling second circuit. Kauto Star fell four fences out when under pressure and then Denman cracked. Imperial Commander had shown glimpses of his resolve when going down to Kauto Star by a nose over 3 miles at Haydock in the autumn and he was a worthy winner. If he stayed the trip, he was a danger to all, and Galway jockey Paddy Brennan said as much by telling the crowd to 'shush' with his finger as he passed the winning post.

The Gold Cup is a race that I get, probably because the bigger the race, the more my pride increases if I tip the winner of it. Isn't that the same for everyone? I can hear Profit frowning in the next room. And that is often the problem with betting. You could say a 3/1 winner at Wolverhampton on the all-weather is the same as a 3/1 winner in the Gold Cup, but it's not the same. If I back a 3/1 winner in the blue riband, the big one, the Gold Cup, it will assist my confidence to look for profit, so it's not a case of me forgetting my rules. The reason is that you should be doing well in your areas of expertise. If I cannot win on the sports I know most about when it comes to betting, then either my strategy is wrong or I am in the wrong frame of mind. I know I am good at the game. Do you?

In the Gold Cup I have tipped two second-placed finishers (Truckers Tavern at 33/1 in 2003, Sir Rembrandt at 40/1 in 2004) and one third-placed finisher (Turpin Green at 66/1 in 2007), at massive prices each way because the race is about staying, and sometimes the classier horses can get beaten by hardier types. On the other hand, I have given some dunderhead investment-advice this decade, remaining loyal to Beef or Salmon in the Gold Cup when he never won a race in Britain, took a horrible fall on his first visit to Cheltenham and was never a fluent jumper at pace on quick ground. Every time he ran in Ireland, Beef or Salmon would perform miracles – beating Best Mate, winning flat races. He hated Cheltenham, and it took me longer to realise that than it should have.

What else do we need to know about the Gold Cup? Well, sixteen of the last seventeen winners were aged between seven and nine. The last ten winners had won a Grade 1 Chase. All but one of the last ten winners had won or finished second at a previous Cheltenham Festival. You need to closely examine the results of the King George Chase at Kempton on St Stephen's Day, the Lexus Chase at Leopardstown, the Irish Hennessy at Leopardstown, the Argento Chase at Cheltenham in January and the previous year's RSA Chase. Paul Nicholls has trained four winners of the race since 1999. And, as regards the Irish challenge, Kicking King and War of Attrition did us proud in 2005 and 2006, but before then we went through a period of twenty-six years with only 2 winners (Dawn Run in 1986 and Imperial Call in 1996).

1989 was the nadir for Irish racing, as we returned from Cheltenham with nothing. No winners. Nada. Like now, that was a time when there was an economic crisis, and back then our best-bred horses were being sold overseas. Given Ireland had produced the brilliant Arkle,

Dawn Run, L'Escargot, Hatton's Grace and Cottage Rake to win the top races at Cheltenham over time, it was a humiliating state of affairs. In 1958 we had eight winners and thankfully by 1996, the bad days were over, with seven Irish-trained winners in three days. In 2010 there were also seven winners. In the heady days of Celtic Tiger haze in 2005 and 2006, there were nine and ten Irish-trained winners respectively and in both years we won the Champion Hurdle, Champion Chase and Gold Cup. And the Grand National at Aintree for bonus points.

So those days of us doing our dough on the Irish certainty and enduring an abject week are over. Or are they?

**The Supreme Novices' Hurdle (Tuesday, 2 miles)** is the first of the supplementary races to have a word about. It's the first race of the meeting. And once the tremendous roar goes up from the crowd for the start of Cheltenham, your fate is now in the lap of the gods. What you will immediately note is the pace at which the horses travel. They go at breakneck speed from the start, so if you have been watching races run at a crawl in Ireland all winter, then you may be surprised. Cheltenham pace over the minimum distance of 2 miles suits horses that possess a blend of speed and stamina. The term the Irish Banker has such negative connotations nowadays that I'm almost afraid to type it, but at Cheltenham it means the horse from our shores which cannot lose, which will give us our bank of betting booty for the week and guarantee our fund for Aintree, Fairyhouse and Punchestown. Istabraq and

Danoli played the part to perfection in the 1990s, but the Supreme Novices' Hurdle has been a graveyard for sure things carrying Irish money. Dunguib in 2010, at 4/5, was the latest over-hyped horse to come a cropper. It's a good race for the Irish, with seven wins from the last ten runnings, but Cousin Vinny, Youlneverwalkalone and Finnegan's Hollow have started favourite in the green-white-and-gold corner and got done. Seven winners of this race have returned a starting price of over 20/1 in the last quarter of a century. Nine of the last ten winners were primed, as they had run in the previous seven weeks. As Irish-trained beasts do so well, put in your ledger the winners of the Royal Bond Hurdle at Fairyhouse in December and the Novices' Hurdle at Leopardstown on Hennessy Day in February.

**The Arkle Chase (Tuesday, 2 miles)** is often won by a former top hurdler. Sizing Europe – a former Champion Hurdle favourite, won in 2010. You need a good jumper at speed – Gold Cup winners Kicking King and War of Attrition were beaten in this race as youngsters. So look for a horse who has run in a decent trial. Don't be put off by long shots – there have only been two winning favourites in the last twenty years, but in the last twenty-five years, only two of the winners failed to finish either first or second on their most recent start.

**The William Hill Handicap Chase (Tuesday, 3 miles)** is a good trends race, in that horses aged eleven or older are not competitive (which in other words means they are not worthy of consideration), the last ten winners have had a weight of under 11 stone, and six of the last eight winners won last time out. They included 33/1 shot Chief Dan George, who took the prize in 2010. And he was a former Grade 1 Hurdle winner over the distance at Aintree, so do some detective work. Novices can be competitive – three novices have won this race since 2004.

**The Cross Country Race (Tuesday, 3 miles 7 furlongs)** is a handicap, but weight is not the most important factor. Yes, 25/1 winner A New Story was receiving stones from the top two in the market, Garde Champetre and L'Ami in 2010, but what brought him into calculations was that he was one of the last twenty winners of cross-country races at Cheltenham to have previous experience of the event. Cross-country races are run over all types of fences and up and down banks, so you need a horse who knows the format. Limerick's Enda Bolger is the king of these races and he's trained four of the six Festival winners since its inception in March of 2005. The other two winners were also Irish trained. Forget about horses under the age of eight.

I'm skipping the Mares' Race (there have only been three runnings of it) on the Tuesday and moving to the **National Hunt Chase (Wednesday, 4 miles)**. This race is restricted to novices and amateur riders. Native Emperor in 2004 is the only favourite to have won this race in the last seventeen runnings and there's only been one winner younger than seven since 1990. Jonjo O'Neill's runners must be examined. He won the race three years running between 2002 and 2004 and again in 2007.

The **Neptune Novices' Hurdle (Wednesday, 2½ miles)** is the middle-distance hurdle for novices. Concentrate on horses aged five or six, who finished first or second last time out, as both trends are very strong for this race. Trainer Willie Mullins has a decent record in the race, but Nicky Henderson does not. 2010 winner Peddlers Cross was a point-to-point winner in Ireland who entered the race unbeaten. The majority of recent winners had Irish point-to-point or bumper experience.

The **RSA Chase (Wednesday, 3 miles)** is the Gold Cup for novices. An interesting statistic is that eight of the last ten winners were seven-year-olds. Weapons Amnesty, the 10/1 winner in 2010, was a course and distance winner at Cheltenham. You need a horse with experience – the last ten winners all had at least three chase runs behind them in the season. There has not been a winner older than eight in nineteen years.

The **Coral Cup (Wednesday, 2½ miles)** is a handicap with a maximum field of twenty-eight, so there are no prisoners taken. You have to look at lowly weighted types in handicaps – seven of the last ten winners of this race have carried under 11 stone. Three of the last eight winners have been Irish-trained. Six of the last eight winners won last time out. Spirit River won this at 14/1 in 2010 and was well fancied in February's Totesport

Trophy, a big handicap hurdle at Newbury, before making a mistake. He made amends where it mattered.

I have already referred to Sanctuaire, who won the Fred Winter Juvenile Hurdle at 4/1 in 2010, so let's talk about the **Champion Bumper (Wednesday, 2 miles)**. This championship flat race attracts a huge Irish interest, because we have won fourteen of the eighteen runnings since it was added to the Cheltenham roster in 1992. Maybe it was a way for the course executive to guarantee us a winner back then, when things weren't so good. Cue Card was a 40/1 English-trained shock in 2010, leaving a lot of Irish punters in sombre mood.

This race carries so much hype because bumpers are held at the end of every Irish jumps card and horses bound for Cheltenham may run less than three times before travelling. Bumpers are run far less frequently in England. Bumpers bring a lot to the game: the uncertainty is a positive; the bullshit chatter is a negative. There's always some yard's bumper horse that is the next superstar, but it is difficult to measure the quality of one race against another because most horses don't run side by side until Cheltenham. Look for a last-time-out winner, as sixteen of the eighteen had won their previous start. Willie Mullins is the bumper king – he's won the race six times. Cue Card was the first four-year-old winner since 1995, so I would side with five and six-year-olds. And for crying out loud, because the evidence on the form book is scant, keep your head screwed on with the money you put down on this race. We don't all get

'Dunguib'-style information. I backed Hairy Molly to win in 2006 at 40/1 on the morning of the race. He won. But I still don't know how I did it.

The **Jewson Novices' Handicap Chase (Thursday, 2½ miles)** has a very interesting history. Trainers are trying to get their horse in on a decent weight – and the evidence is that all six winners of this race had won only once over fences. However, all of them came into the race in form, finishing first or second last time out. Copper Bleu won this in 2010 at 12/1. He had course form – he was fourth in a Supreme Novices' Hurdle. (From 2011, this race will be renamed the Centenary Novices' Handicap Chase. There will be a new Jewson Novices' Chase over the same trip of 2½ miles, a level-weights race, in distance between the 2-mile Arkle Chase and the 3-mile RSA Chase.)

The **Pertemps Final (Thursday, 3 miles)** has been a good race for the Irish, with five winners in the last eighteen runnings. Like the World Hurdle, you need to forget about five-year-olds at this distance as there hasn't been a five-year-old winner since 1988. All of the winners bar one have carried less than 10 stone 9 pounds since 2004. Watch out for runners in the silks of owner JP McManus – he's had two winners (Creon, 2004 and Kadoun, 2006) at 50/1 in the last decade. The last seven winners of this race started at double figure prices.

The **Ryanair Chase (Thursday, 2½ miles)** is the race for horses which are not fast enough for the Champion

Chase and don't have enough stamina for the Gold Cup. 2½ miles is a Goldilocks Optimum. Since this race came into being in 2005, all six winners had previous wins on the board at Cheltenham. Keep an eye out for French-bred horses, as they do well in chases up to this trip at Cheltenham and bear in mind those trained by Paul Nicholls, as he already has two wins in this race.

**The Byrne Group Plate (Thursday, 2½ miles)** used to be known as the Mildmay of Flete Handicap Chase. It should be known as the Bookies' Benefit, because the last ten winners have started at double-figure prices. No massive gambles have been landed by punters in this race. Eight of the last ten winners carried under 11 stone, and all but two of the last nineteen winners finished no worse than fourth on their most recent outing. There has only been one Irish-trained winner in sixty years, which is shocking. Why? In my mind, it's because we have a paucity of handicap chases run at a decent pace before the Irish meetings at Fairyhouse and Punchestown. And the top Irish chasers go for the level weights Graded events, such as the Arkle or the Ryanair Chase.

The **Kim Muir Chase (Thursday, 3 miles)** is a handicap chase for amateur riders. Immediately check if the silks of owner Trevor Hemmings (green, yellow and white) are anywhere to be found, because he has owned three of the last six winners. All but two of the last ten winners have been eight or nine-year-olds. Weight is not a major factor in this race. Trainers Nicky Henderson and

Ferdy Murphy have decent histories in the race, but Paul Nicholls does not. Another bad race for the Irish, with no winner trained in the Emerald Isle since 1983. I refer you to the comments about the Byrne Group Plate.

The **Triumph Hurdle (Friday, 2 miles)** is a race I used to hate, but they've improved it with the introduction of the **Fred Winter Juvenile Hurdle**, which takes some of the lesser types out of this race. The Triumph Hurdle is confined to four-year-old juveniles and most entrants have flat-racing experience in France, England or Ireland before embarking on a career over jumps. Cheltenham tests a horse's stamina more than other speedier tracks over 2 miles, so forget about horses that don't have form over at least 1 mile 4 furlongs on the flat. Soldatino, the 2010 winner at 6/1, had winning flat form over 1 mile 6 furlongs. He was trainer Nicky Henderson's fifth winner in twenty-six years, but there hasn't been an Irish winner since 2002. Side with last time out winners. Despite my current doubts about his flock, trainer Alan King has a decent record in this race.

The **County Hurdle (Friday, 2 miles)** used to be the last race of the Festival – now it's the appetiser before the Gold Cup. It remains a cavalry charge. 2010 winner Thousand Stars, a 20/1 winner, was one of four Irish winners in the last eight years, so keep an eye on the big Leopardstown handicaps. Seven of the last ten winners of the County carried under 11 stone and you need a gutsy animal. Have on your side a horse with at least four runs in the season. Trainer Paul Nicholls has a good recent record in the race.

There are not enough trends for my liking to size up the 3-mile Novices' Hurdle, or the new 2½ mile Conditional Jockeys Handicap Hurdle, so I will conclude with two races. The **Foxhunter Chase (Friday, 3¼ miles)** is run over the Gold Cup distance after the race itself. It's for amateur riders and although licensed trainers may enter, the horse must have at least some type of hunting experience outside traditional courses. Baby Run, who was the 9/2 winner in 2010, was third in the race in 2009, so he had proven course form. A lot of OAP's turn up in this race, but eighteen of the last twenty winners have been ten or younger. And 80% of the runners over the last quarter of the century won last time out. The Irish record in this isn't great with Whyso Mayo in 2006 the only winner in the last ten runnings.

The **Grand Annual (Friday, 2 miles)** is the final race of the Festival. Keep an eye on Arthur Moore's horses, as he's won it twice in the last decade. Focus on horses younger than ten. The last ten winners carried under 11 stone. As this is another furious affair in terms of pace, look to horses with winning form over further than 2 miles. Pigeon Island won this at 16/1 in 2010. He had winning course form but more importantly he liked soft ground, which the horses were running on after a deluge of rain all afternoon. Racing opened with the ground described as good. I layed Tartak – a good-ground horse – in this race. Tartak ran well for a long way but faded into fifth in the mud. An example from the biggest meeting of the racing year why you should show your hand late when betting on any horse race.

## Strike Rates

When you set aside your betting fund for Cheltenham or any other race meeting, you may feel confident that you have completed your homework. You may feel you have all the angles covered in terms of the races themselves, but do you know the performance of trainers and jockeys at the course in the most recent years? A strike rate is the ratio of winners to runners.

When you analyse the strike rate for Cheltenham in particular over the last five National Hunt seasons, you will see Paul Nicholls at the top of the pile in terms of winners at the course for all the meetings held there (not just March). Nicholls was also the top trainer at the Festival between 2006 and 2009. However, at the time of writing in November 2010, Nicholls has a losing strike rate at Cheltenham, in that if you placed a pound on each of his runners at all course meetings over the last five seasons, you would suffer a loss of just over £100.

Nigel Twiston-Davies trained three winners at the 2010 Festival, but more importantly his overall strike rate at Cheltenham is very positive – backing all of his runners to a £1 stake in the last five seasons would have generated a profit of over £60. Twiston-Davies nearly gave up the game around 2002 – he has now trained a total of 13 Festival winners, including six in the last three years.

Nicky Henderson is the king of Festival training – with thirty-seven winners to his name over the past quarter of a century. Nicholls comes next on twenty-seven, Ireland's Edward O'Grady has notched eighteen successes, while Jonjo O'Neill and Willie Mullins lie on seventeen. O'Grady has been quiet in recent years, but Mullins hasn't. Mullins has trained seven Festival winners over the past three years, and his strike rate for all runners at Cheltenham is a positive £18 to a £1 level stake. Donald McCain has really impressed with three winners in the last three Festivals, while Emma Lavelle has sent out two winners from a small yard. I would stay on the right side of David Pipe at Cheltenham going forward – he had two winners at 16/1 and 18/1 in 2010, and his father Martin always had a horse ready for one of the handicaps. Ferdy Murphy's runners must also be noted. In 2006 Murphy trained Hot Weld and You're Special to win at 33/1, and then in 2007 he sent out L'Antartique and Joe's Edge to win at prices of 20/1 and 50/1 respectively. Poker De Sivola's win at 14/1 in the 4-mile chase in 2010 means that Murphy is showing a tidy Cheltenham profit over the last five seasons. Nick Williams, Thomas Cooper and Gordon Elliott are three other names for the notebook but, as I mentioned earlier, I am wary of Alan King and Noel Meade when it comes to Cheltenham. King doesn't seem to have the firepower that he once had and Meade, for a multiple-winning champion trainer in Ireland, has only tasted victory at the Festival three times in his twenty-year career, which is a very poor return and a real loss-maker for the blind follower.

As for jockeys, Tony McCoy is a machine and has brought the sport into the mainstream, but his Cheltenham successes have been few and far between of late. Barry Geraghty has the benefit of being Henderson's stable jockey and a well-connected freelance who rides in Ireland, so his profitable strike rate of £30 shouldn't surprise anyone. Ruby Walsh has ridden twenty-seven Cheltenham Festival winners, which is more than anyone else in history – and the Kildare man is showing a small profit to a level stake in recent years.

# Chapter 8

## *The Grand National, Fairyhouse, Punchestown and Galway*

Betting is a great leveller. One day the potential outcome may be crystal clear in your mind, the next day you cannot get a handle on what might happen. Confidence and confusion can go hand in hand and that was the case with my experience of the **Aintree Grand National** from one year to the next. Listening back to my tip on Comply or Die at 10/1 two days before the start of the 2008 race, I can hear supreme confidence. I really felt I had found The One. Comply or Die, trained by David Pipe, was a smart novice chaser, who had finished second in the RSA Chase at Cheltenham in 2005. The horse then lost his way, but I felt if he was back to his best, he would take some beating. Pipe had applied blinkers to help the horse concentrate and he had a lovely racing weight of 10 stone 9 pounds. Timmy Murphy, a very decent chase jockey, was on board.

I usually have a main bet on 'The National' and a

small nibble on another horse. The nibble in 2008 was on Mon Mome. This horse finished second in the Welsh National in 2006 and I guessed he might be suited to the extra 7 furlongs at Aintree. My faith in Comply or Die was justified, as the horse jumped like buck and surged clear to win under Murphy. I must have watched the repeat ten times that evening. Mon Mome struggled home in tenth place, beaten 58 lengths. A year later, Mon Mome started at 100/1 for the Grand National. Mon Mome was trained by Venetia Williams and had won a good race at Cheltenham the previous winter. But he was a disappointing eighth in the subsequent Welsh National, and given his performance at Aintree twelve months before, I couldn't fancy him. I thus carried a very puzzled expression when Mon Mome broke from the pack after the final fence and sprinted home to become the first 100/1 winner of the Grand National since Foinavon in 1967. That's racing. That's sport. You think you have everything worked out and then what you least expect materialises before your very eyes.

The Grand National, which takes place in Liverpool on a Saturday in early April, is *the* race which brings the sport into our conversations and living rooms. For 364 days a year, many are oblivious to jockeys, fallers, weight and gambles, but the National, the richest steeplechase in the world, is the annual event to which the people decide they want to belong. And the people put the money down in their millions to find one winner from forty brave horses as the drama unfolds over 4½ miles and thirty big fences.

Witnessing the reaction of the best jumps jockey of our generation, Tony McCoy, when he finally won the Grand National at the fifteenth attempt in 2010, brought it home to those who didn't know what it means to the racing fraternity. Sir Peter O'Sullevan, the voice of racing, and one of the best sports commentators to ever walk the earth, captivated the audience for years with his mellifluous tones, building his pitch to a crescendo as the horses jumped the final flight and then ran for home on our screens. The great Michael O'Hehir was there in 1967 to see Foinavon skip past a pile-up of horses and, in 2001, Jim McGrath commentated on a race in atrocious conditions when Red Marauder and Smarty were the only horses left standing in a race in which thirty-eight horses fell.

The first Grand National was staged in 1839 and won by a horse called Lottery, and there is a prevailing sense among both the man on the street and the racing experts that the race is just that – a lottery. I've backed horses properly every year in the Grand National since 1997 and, in spite of Mon Mome, I've made a profit on it. I believe a very specific type of horse is required to win the race and a lot of the field can be ruled out of your calculations before they begin the marathon. Of course luck is required and that's natural when we're talking about many horses attempting to jump the unique and daunting fences over a distance longer than any other race in the UK and Ireland. There are many fallers, but not many Grand National winners could be described as fluke winners.

Aintree is a flat, left-handed course. There are two tracks at Aintree: the Grand National Course and the Mildmay Course which stages the regular races over the three-day meeting. The Grand National has changed in modern times. The fences are not as severe as they used to be, which has a lot to do with the British Horseracing Board being keen to avoid the negative press that goes with horse fatalities. The ground is always watered before the Aintree meeting, which prevents the surface from becoming too fast – thus acting as a preventative mechanism against deaths. And the very best chasers often avoid the race, unlike in the 1970s, when Cheltenham Gold Cup winner L'Escargot and Champion Chase winner Crisp tried their luck. The absence of such leading lights as Kauto Star and Denman in recent times guarantees that all horses run off their correct rating in what remains, for all intents and purposes, a handicap chase.

So what qualities does a horse require to win the Grand National? The first thing the horse must do is jump well. I won't win the Nobel Prize for stating that, but the fences, packed with spruce, take jumping, especially in soft ground. Some of the obstacles, at 5 foot, are bigger and constructed differently from normal racecourse fences. Therefore some horses enjoy them and some don't. The most famous fence is called Becher's Brook, which is jumped twice in the race (sixth and twenty-second fences). The issue with Becher's is not the fence itself, but the steep drop below which can catch a horse out. The fence has been modified over the years and is much easier now, but it remains a tricky obstacle. The Chair (the fifteenth) is only jumped once and that's the biggest fence on the course. West Tip (1985) fell at Becher's Brook and Silver Birch (2006) fell at The Chair in the years before their victories, so even the best horses can fall. A sketchy jumper will not only struggle to get around, but will also lose vital ground at fences to better jumpers, which counts double in a race over 4½ miles. I can only remember two poor jumpers winning the Grand National, Maori Venture in 1987 (the horse had a great engine and got away with some sloppy leaps) and Red Marauder in 2001 (he was able to somehow climb over the fences in that heavy ground).

I referred to the distance of the race because when you consider the Grand National trip of 4 miles 4 furlongs, you need to ask yourself, "Does the horse stay the trip?" Since 1970 no horse has ever won the Grand National without winning a previous race over three miles. That's forty-one years of data, so get out the form book. Often you see horses up with the pace for the first circuit of the race, only to see them fade approaching the finish. Therefore you should examine the horse's career form, not just its most recent performances. Has it performed well in any of the long-distance trials over 3 miles, such as the Hennessy Gold Cup at Newbury, the Welsh National at Chepstow, or a previous Irish National at Fairyhouse? I backed Slim Pickings in the 2007 race because I knew he was a decent traveller in his races, jumped well and had a low weight. And he was going as well as anything else three fences from home before Silver Birch flew past him by The Elbow and stayed on to win. So Slim Pickings ran well to finish third, but he didn't stay well enough to win. The same can be said about Big Fella Thanks in 2010. By watching the race, you could see he stayed 4 miles, but not 4½. So the margins can be tight, even for the longest race of all.

The third consideration when approaching a selection for the Grand National is the weight the horse is carrying. Between 1983 and 2009, only Hedgehunter in 2005 carried over 11 stone. And in winning the race in 2010, Don't Push It became the first horse since Red Rum in the 1970s to win the race carrying at least 11 stone 5 pounds. The reason weight is so important in the Grand National is because of the distance of the race. As we know, the Grand National is a handicap, which means that a horse with a theoretically better ability will carry top weight, or 11 stone 10 pounds, while a theoretically weaker horse can carry anything down to 10 stone. The weights are decided by taking into account the previous runs of a horse and then determined for each runner so that each of the forty should have an equal chance. We are dealing with horses here, not humans, but the overlying trend has been that lowly weighted horses have a better chance of winning the Grand National. I must flag that the British Handicapper, or the man who decides the weights, has in recent years aimed to attract the bigger names or classier types to race in the Grand National by giving them a few pounds less at the top of the handicap than they would ordinarily carry. And that's one of the reasons Don't Push It was able to win despite carrying

11 stone 5 pounds in 2010. This was a horse that ran very close to Gold Cup winner Denman as a novice, so weight could not stop his class from winning out.

There are other pointers to note. You need a horse with experience to win the Grand National. A seven-year-old has not won the race since Bogskar in 1940. You need to be looking within the eight to twelve-year age bracket for winners, as older horses find the exacting trip easier to handle. Also, look at the breeding of the horse. Mon Mome has been the only French-bred winner of the Grand National in a hundred years. That's because French-bred horses are in training at a younger age and often peak a lot earlier, with their best years between the ages of five and nine. Also, French-bred horses are usually tried at trips up to 3 miles, so their pedigrees are not exactly suited to marathon distances.

The Irish drought at Aintree spanned twenty-four years, from L'Escargot's win in 1975 to Bobbyjo's victory in 1999. Much of that time in the doldrums was a result of Irish racing playing second fiddle to its English cousin, but since 1999 there have been six Irish-trained winners. Bobbyjo's success was a brilliant piece of training by Tommy Carberry, who managed to get a horse that had won the previous year's Irish National into the race out of the handicap with just 10 stone, after running Bobbyjo over hurdles to protect his mark. And you can watch the race to see the rest.

So let's take a look back, from 1997 on, when I first seriously became 'involved' in the Grand National, to identify the trends which keep repeating themselves.

**1997 Lord Gyllene:** This New Zealand-bred horse won by 25 lengths, which wasn't a surprise, as he was only off 10 stone, instead of the big weight he carried in the Grand National trial at Uttoxeter. And his previous form had shown him to be a fantastic jumper, so he was made for the race. You'll never get a better winner at 14/1.

**1998 Earth Summit:** This horse went off the 7/1 favourite in heavy ground and everything pointed to a victory beforehand. He had won the Scottish and Welsh Grand Nationals, was carrying only 10 stone 5 pounds and had proven form in the conditions.

**1999 Bobbyjo:** I didn't back him, but this horse had won the previous year's Irish Grand National off a weight of 11 stone 3, so the quality was there to see. Not a shock.

**2000 Papillon:** I remember studying this race for hours the night before and then it just struck me. Papillon was The One. I took the 20/1 the next morning, before the horse was backed down to 10/1. This winner never fell in his life, had finished a narrow second to Bobbyjo in the 1998 Irish National and was carrying a reasonable weight of 10 stone 12 pounds. He'd also been shrewdly entered by trainer Ted Walsh in some of the top 2-mile races, so there was no problem with him travelling comfortably for a long way.

And Ruby Walsh arrived on the scene in some style with the incredible ride he gave the winner. It was his first ride in the race.

**2001 Red Marauder:** This race was staged in the worst ground I have ever seen at a racecourse, so the result was a bit of a freak. However, there was no doubt about Red Marauder's ability to handle heavy ground. He had finished fifth, staying on at the end of the race in similar conditions in the Hennessy Gold Cup over 3¼ miles at Newbury earlier that season.

**2002 Bindaree:** I backed this horse in the 2001 Welsh National and he finished third. An eight-year-old winner at 20/1, he was a good novice hurdler. A surprise, but his trainer had won the race before and he was given an amazing spin by Jim Culloty, who literally threw this fellow from pillar to post.

**2003 Monty's Pass:** This horse had form over the Aintree fences, with a second in the Topham Chase over a shorter trip in 2002. He then won the Kerry National under a big weight en route to Aintree. A brilliant jumper, he had a nice low weight and didn't touch a twig under jockey Barry Geraghty.

**2004 Amberleigh House:** A really decent chaser in Ireland, this horse was sent to Ginger McCain to win the National – and he did at the age of twelve. Amberleigh won the Becher Chase in 2001 over the same fences and finished third in the race behind Monty's Pass in 2003.

**2005 Hedgehunter:** Hedgehunter blazed a trail for a long way in the 2004 race, before a tired fall at the last fence. A year later, he turned up a stronger horse and won easily under Ruby Walsh for trainer Willie Mullins.

**2006 Numbersixvalverde:** This horse benefited from a cool waiting ride by Niall 'Slippers' Madden on rain-softened ground which suited his ability to stay longer than the mother-in-law. This horse won the previous year's Irish Grand National over the stiff Fairyhouse fences.

**2007 Silver Birch:** This was a dream day for trainer Gordon Elliott, who won his fourth race in Britain in the National with Silver Birch. Elliott never gave up on this horse, who had battled serious leg problems. Before all that, he had won the Becher Chase over the same fences and taken the Welsh National when with trainer Paul Nicholls.

**2008 Comply or Die** and **2009 Mon Mome:** See above.

**2010 Don't Push It:** This wasn't just a win for McCoy. The horse gave trainer Jonjo O'Neill and owner JP McManus their first victory in the famous race. I had a feeling approaching the day that I didn't have my finger on the winner. It was intuition. I couldn't see the wood for the trees. My tip, Arbor Supreme, fell at The Chair, which in retrospect wasn't too surprising, as he had his own ideas about jumping. I was a little put off by the weight Don't Push It was carrying, and felt some horse below him in the handicap would be too good. I've already vouched for the horse's class and he ran well when a fast-finishing second at Cheltenham in a race over a mile shorter than the Grand National in November 2009. A very important point in analysing the win of Don't Push It was that he had winning course form at Aintree. It wasn't over the Grand National fences, but it was winning form at the track nonetheless.

**Aintree** and Punchestown are decent festivals, but as full meetings they are in the shadow of Cheltenham and the results from Cheltenham do have an impact upon them. Denman, Kauto Star and Imperial Commander have all started favourite for Aintree's 'Gold Cup' – **The Totesport Bowl** on the Thursday – and all three have been beaten. Horses are trained to peak at certain times, so that's why there's only been one Cheltenham winner from the same season to grace the National winners billboard since 1961. For trivia buffs it was Seagram in 1991. That's one Cheltenham winner to follow up in the big race in fifty years! There's also a laser-like focus from Irish trainers on Cheltenham, so we have to go back to 2002 and Florida Pearl for the last Irish Totesport Bowl winner. **The Melling Chase** at Aintree takes place over

2½ miles on the Friday and once again, Cheltenham runners such as Well Chief and Master Minded have started at odds-on in the betting and suffered defeat. The distance caught them out, so check Ryanair Chase winners from Cheltenham. The 2010 Melling winner, Albertas Run, had won the Ryanair Chase, but still started at a tasty 8/1. The Melling Chase also suits older horses, as all but one of the last ten winners were eight years of age or older. To conclude my point about Cheltenham and Aintree, trainer Nicky Henderson has trained the last two winners of the Champion Hurdle at Cheltenham, but he has never won the 2½ mile **Aintree Hurdle** on the Saturday. This is a race in which Irish horses do well. We have won six of the last eight runnings, with Al Eile, a course specialist, taking home the silver three times.

There are two races at Aintree that are run over one circuit of the National fences before the big race. They are **The Foxhunters Chase** on the Thursday and **The Topham Chase** on the Friday. The distance for these races is 2 miles 5 furlongs and you must have a prominent racer who jumps well in each race. Horses just do not come from behind to win over these fences. Note that, unlike Cheltenham, experience is needed for the Foxhunters. All winners have been nine or older in the last ten runnings. In the Topham, horses older than ten have a dreadful record. The Topham is a handicap, so pick those carrying less than 11 stone. It's also a bonus if they have previous experience over the fences.

In terms of strike rates at Aintree, if recent evidence is anything to go by, seek out the runners trained by

Peter Bowen. Bowen, who is based in Wales, has a remarkable profit figure of over £130 to a £1 stake from his runners in Liverpool over the last five seasons. He's also trained two of the last four winners of the Topham Chase at double-figure prices. Howard Johnson loves Aintree and has his fair share of winners, but his strike rate is negative. Jonjo O'Neill's is positive, but Paul Nicholls' is negative.

**Fairyhouse** stages the **Irish Grand National** on Easter Monday every year and while it doesn't hold the same attention as its English counterpart, it is a fine race. Desert Orchid came over to win it in 1990, and there have been a surprising number of Aintree winners who were also victorious in our version e.g. Rhyme 'N' Reason, Bobbyjo and Numbersixvalverde. The Irish National is held over a distance of 3 miles 5 furlongs. Fairyhouse is a right-handed track and relatively flat, although the fences can be tough to jump. I really feel you need a lightly weighted horse in any National and the evidence at Fairyhouse supports this. The last ten winners have carried under 11 stone. The 2010 winner, a 25/1 outsider called Bluesea Cracker, only had 10 stone 4 on her back. This mare had a previous win at the course to her name, which was important and her form was closely matched with the Leopardstown Paddy Power Chase winner Oscar Time, who would finish second to her in the Irish National. She had won over 3 miles and while she was inconsistent, you could have given her a chance. She was in the right age bracket, because most Irish National winners are aged between seven and nine. Rhyme 'N' Reason was the last six-year-old to win, twenty-six years ago. Of the last ten winners, only Granit D'Estruval was older than nine. Willie Mullins, Ireland's leading trainer, has never won the Irish National. The English record in recent times is decent, with three winners since 2004, so I wouldn't put you off a visitor. And don't be afraid to pick an outsider – in the last seven years there have been three 33/1 winners, a 25/1 success and a victor at 20/1.

**Punchestown** is the Irish National Hunt Festival and they have done a fantastic job in recent years of attracting sponsors and English trainers and owners. It was also a clever move of them to start the meetings in late afternoon. In 2011 it will be held in early May, and they water the ground sufficiently to make it safe for jumpers. It's a well-run meeting, lasting from Tuesday to Saturday, but it can be exhausting if you get heavily involved as a punter.

Punchestown is right-handed and undulating, but not as stiff a course as Cheltenham. I tend to find that it is worth following horses that travel up with the pace at this Kildare venue – and because English horses are in the minority, look to Irish horses who have met earlier in the season to guide your form study in the Graded races. If you are getting involved in Punchestown, you need to check who Willie Mullins has entered in the races. In 2009 and 2010 he trained twelve winners at each meeting which was nothing short of sensational. In

2010, Mullins ran fifty-three horses. If you had placed €1 on each of the fifty-three horses to win only, you would have collected €96.38. That is a serious profit. Now obviously, Mullins had an incredible week and is unlikely to repeat it, but that's what we said in 2010 after 2009. The lesson is that a yard in red-hot form is likely to maintain that level of form for the duration of a Festival. I like Mullins because every horse in the stable has a chance. By the Friday, in four days he had already trained seven winners and then he sent out a 25/1 outsider from his *own* stable, Palace Merano, to win.

It's wise to note the upcoming trainers who will be the champions of the future. Willie Mullins is well established, but has yet to win one of the big races at the Cheltenham Festival. I expect that to change in the coming years. Trends apply to Punchestown like everywhere else. In the Gold Cup, the feature race on the Wednesday, English horses have won three of the last four runnings and the jolly (the favourite) has taken this in seven of the last ten years. From an age perspective, all of the winners since 2004 have been eight or younger. Beef or Salmon was more suited to Punchestown than Cheltenham when he won in 2004, but Denman couldn't handle going right-handed in 2010. In the Champion Chase on the Tuesday, French-breds have won the last four runnings of the event and, since 2000, eight of the runnings have gone to eight or nine-year-olds. In the Champion Hurdle on the Friday, you need to select an in-form horse. 2007 winner Silent

Oscar was 20/1, but came into the race off a good win on the flat. Five-year-olds have a better record in this race than in the Champion Hurdle at Cheltenham. In the Champion Bumper on the Wednesday, pick out the horses which won last time out, because seven of the last ten have. Also, Noel Meade has trained the winner of the race three times since 2004 and ten of the last twelve winners had only three runs or less going into the race.

## Galway

Park benches, pink euro notes, white shoes, Animal Lover (name of a horse). These are some of the images I remember from my one and only trip to the Galway Races. I don't think I will ever go back. Galway is high octane and very social. Cheltenham is enough for me. Over 150,000 people travelled to hell or to Connacht for the seven days in 2010, and the bookmakers reported turnover of €100 million in the recession. Yes, Galway is a big deal and I have mixed feelings about it. If Cheltenham is the Olympics or the GAA Championship of horse-racing, Galway is the People's Week. The racing is a mixed bag – some of it is pretty poor – but the track at Ballybrit is decent, albeit quirky. The idea to mix flat and jump-racing works and the timing of the Festival around the August Bank Holiday weekend suits the diaries of many. In recent years the Galway Races was associated with haughtiness and helicopters, but the Festival was first held in 1869 and like all fads, that has passed and it has begun to regain its flavour as a burger, iceberger, fake-tan and pint week. Galway is very democratic. The high rollers and the down-at-heel are equal there, and it's not only the horses that need stamina, with the activity in the town and at the track. My father used to take his holidays specifically to go to the Galway Races. I don't know how many spouses would allow that kind of carry-on these days.

I have already told you how I ran home 'crying to mommy' after Galway in 2003. Between 2003 and 2005, I would come off a respectable Cheltenham and dread having to give charity tips on the Galway Plate and the Galway Hurdle, as the horses would summarily start running towards the Atlantic Ocean under a motionless jockey (called 'on the bridle') rather than the third last fence. I couldn't get my head around it. I hated it. And I think my messy week in '03 had clouded my mind. Then I tipped the 2006 Galway Plate winner Far From Trouble at 8/1; the 2007 Galway Plate winner Sir Frederick at 12/1; the 2008 Galway Hurdle winner Indian Pace at 11/1; and in the 2009 Galway Plate, I put up Knock On The Head at 16/1 and Anothercoppercoast at 25/1 and both were placed.

So given the turnaround in personal fortunes, what's the best advice to make money out West? The key to Galway, if you are going to play, is to look for the nuances, because this meeting, at a much greater level than any other race meeting, is about trainers gearing their horses to show their best form on the day in order to win a big pot, both in terms of prize money and in the betting ring. Owners and trainers target Cheltenham too, but it's very hard to win there, and while middling horses can win at Galway, they have no chance against the equine superstars trained during the regular jumps season between November and April by Messrs Nicholls, Henderson and Mullins at Cheltenham.

Instead of concentrating on superstars, because that's not what Galway is about, it's best to zone in on certain elements – the top trainer Mr Dermot Weld, the Galway Plate over fences, which is the first big race of the week, and the Galway Hurdle, which is the other big race of the week.

Now, Dermot Weld. That's the name you should remember if you are going to the Galway Races, or going to place a bet at the Galway Races in the coming years. I am writing this the day after the 2010 Festival at Ballybrit, where Weld was crowned champion trainer for the 26th time.

Weld is a great trainer. Any man who sends a horse to Australia to win a Melbourne Cup (Vintage Crop in 1993) and then wins the race again (Media Puzzle in 2002) knows the time of day. Weld has also trained two Irish Derby winners amid a clean sweep of the domestic Classics on the flat, a Belmont Stakes winner in the USA and an English 2000 Guineas winner. Weld is Galway. Every year he prepares for Ballybrit with military precision and every year he cleans up. Until his form recedes or he retires, he should be your first port of call. Obviously, the bookmakers factor this into the equation when announcing their prices, but if you had put €1 each way on all of Weld's thirty-three runners in 2010, you would have made a profit of nearly €23 from a €66 outlay, a profit of 34 per cent.

I couldn't believe that Weld's first runner at Galway 2010 won at 5/1. Did people even notice his record at the course or were they too busy chatting up pints in the bar? The next day, he sent out the winner of a big 2-mile flat handicap, Eazy Mate, at 12/1. On the Saturday, his bumper horse won at 6/1, taking his tally for the week to 11 winners. And it wasn't as if all of this was a shock. Weld entered Galway 2010 in fine form, having trained Rite of Passage to win the Ascot Gold Cup. It doesn't take hours of research to know what works and what doesn't at Galway or any race meeting – just a bit of reading. So even though a Weld runner may be a relative outsider, as Eazy Mate was, his horses are always worth a look. Sometimes you have to forget about the market. And if you are able to trust your own knowledge, you can also spot when a Weld horse is too short in the betting, as Majestic Concorde, a horse that lacked experience over fences, was for the 2010 Galway Plate. He went off at a ridiculously short 3/1 and finished third. Weld commented on the television beforehand that he just wanted the horse home safe and sound. So he was a horse worth laying. Generally, Weld's historical dominance of Galway is a very big trend to bear in mind when putting down the money. 'Horses for Courses' is a popular phrase. 'Trainers for Courses' should be too. For example, would you lump onto a Dermot Weld runner at Cheltenham? No, because he hasn't had a winner there since 1990.

You can read the *Racing Post* under candlelight until 3 a.m. and have it all worked out and go into work the next day bleary-eyed, having forgotten everything you have read, only for it to return ten minutes before the off. Or you can become so obsessed with the form book that when it's turned on its head at Galway, you can't understand why you bother. I watched Say Again win the 2002 Galway Hurdle at 16/1 and Nearly a Moose take the Plate in 2003 at 25/1 and neither victory made sense on the basis of form, so that fundamentally changed my approach to reading race form. Galway, once again, is often about interpretation of the *best* form, so instead of putting your eggs entirely on the behaviour of the animal, you have to ask yourself "Who owns it?" "Who trains it?" and "Who is riding it?" This applies to every race meeting, but at Galway, I take extra notice. Look for the invisible ink.

Joseph O'Brien is only a teenager, but he is a good young apprentice jockey. He's also Aidan O'Brien's son. As I felt Joseph would be riding some winners for his father in 2010, I put every single horse owned by the O'Brien family into a horse-alert system at the start of the flat season so I would know when they were running and when Joseph might get a winner. It was the lesson I learned from Patrick Mullins and Cousin Vinny, the 12/1 winner of the 2008 Cheltenham Bumper. Although Willie Mullins' stable jockey Ruby Walsh had a ride in the race, looking back it was obvious that Patrick was on the best one, and so it proved, as there were family celebrations in the winners' enclosure. I've already told you about Joseph O'Brien and Lady Lupus, the 200/1 each-way filly at the Curragh. Unfortunately, I was out of the loop and didn't back Joseph O'Brien's horses when the television cameras were whirring at Galway. From ten rides, he rode four winners: a 25/1 outsider; a 14/1 shot; a 9/2 chance and another at 9/4. The 9/4 winner was his first ride of the week for his father. He also had two second-placed finishes, at 10/1 and 3/1. A €1 each way investment on the ten mounts would have handed you a €50 profit on a €20 outlay, or a return of 250%. Not bad going, eh? Galway 2010 was Joseph O'Brien's arrival on the scene, and he did it with a 7lb weight claim.

Okay – so let's examine **The Galway Plate**, which is held each year on the Wednesday. The course is a right-handed track with an uphill finish and two quick fences are to be jumped in the straight. So over the distance of 2 miles 6 furlongs, you need a horse that will stay well and jumps well. It's not too dissimilar to Fairyhouse, but the finish is tougher. The ground at Galway is usually good, and even if there has been a bit of rain, it's summer jumping ground, so you should be looking for horses that prefer top of the ground. My rationale in tipping Far From Trouble in 2006 was that the horse had winning form over the distance, had a touch of class (was placed at the Cheltenham Festival and had beaten Homer Wells, a decent novice, the previous year), had no issues with the ground, was a safe jumper and had a low weight. The reason I put up Sir Frederick a year later was primarily down to the weight he was carrying:

9 stone 10 pounds was a featherweight for a horse that had easily won his previous outing, loved the fast ground, had no issues with the trip and had been mixing it with the best novices. His trainer, Liam Burke, while not a big name, had a big reputation from the point-to-point scene. Looking back at the recent history of this race, only Moscow Express in 1999 (a class horse in his day) and Ansar in 2005 (a course specialist and previous winner) have carried over 11 stone to victory in the Plate. Interestingly, Willie Mullins and Noel Meade, the leading Irish trainers in the regular National Hunt season in recent years, have never won a Galway Plate. Horses cannot be campaigned for twelve months of the year and the winter trainers such as Mullins and Meade are at a disadvantage due to their primary focus on Cheltenham and Punchestown.

In terms of age, horses above the age of ten should be opposed. There hasn't been a winner aged ten or over since 1996. Younger horses are generally improving types and over the medium trip of the Plate they often have something in hand on the older horses that have been exposed to the handicapper. The nine-year-old Finger on the Pulse won the 2010 Galway Plate, giving owner JP McManus, trainer Tom Taaffe and jockey Tony McCoy the spoils. This animal was a 22/1 shot and if you were a disciple of lifetime form, you would know that he won a big handicap over a similar distance at the Cheltenham Festival on good ground in 2008. On the basis of that victory, the horse had class, but then completely lost his way and came into the Plate having either fallen or unshipped his rider on his previous three outings. So there's no way you could have backed the horse with any confidence. Another reason to be a sceptic was the wretched form of Taaffe, who hadn't trained a winner since February. The only item to note was the market. McCoy switched from a non-runner to ride Finger on the Pulse and then the price contracted. The market is right more times than it is wrong.

The English-trained Overturn bucked ten years of trends by becoming the first horse since Quinze in 1999 to carry over 11 stone to victory in **The Galway Hurdle**, which is the main event on the Thursday. The Galway Hurdle is a good race, run over 2 miles, the same distance as the Champion Hurdle at Cheltenham, but it's a handicap, and often won by well-handicapped horses (i.e. those which have not shown their true abilities on the form book). Age isn't really a big factor – Perugino Diamond won as a four-year-old in 2000 and the nine-year-old Sabadilla took the honours in 2003. Wexford trainer Paul Nolan's runners must be respected – he has trained three winners in the last decade. I tipped the John Kiely trained Indian Pace in 2008 because I knew he would stay (he ran well over 12 furlongs on the flat at the Curragh), he had no weight (9 stone 10 pounds) and most importantly, he had beaten Cheltenham winner Silver Jaro in a handicap hurdle at Leopardstown the previous December. Best form is your best friend.

Overturn, the first English winner of the Galway Hurdle since Sagaman in 1991, came into the 2010 race with wins in the Scottish Champion Hurdle and in the 2-mile Northumberland Plate on the flat under his belt. His galloping, front-running style was always going to be suited to Galway and that's how it panned out as he pulverised the field. It was a one-horse race. His win was all down to class. You could imagine Overturn running in the Champion Hurdle at Cheltenham against the top horses off level weights. You could not imagine any other horse in the race doing so, and that's why he went off at only 6/1. Overturn's trainer, Donald McCain, the son of Red Rum's (remember him, folks?) handler Ginger McCain, is gaining a nice reputation. If you had read about Overturn in the industry publications, you would have noticed this horse had a breathing operation to help him in his races. This is the type of small print you must read before signing the betting docket or typing your stake on the screen.

# Chapter 9

## *The Flat*

You have probably heard of Sea the Stars, the Irish champion three-year-old thoroughbred flat horse, the horse who won over distances from 1 mile to 1 mile 4 furlongs in his record year, taking in the prestigious English 2000 Guineas at Newmarket, the Epsom Derby, and the Prix de l'Arc de Triomphe at Longchamp in France during a run of six Group 1 wins in 2009. Ridden by a fifty-year-old, Mick Kinane, for trainer John Oxx, Sea the Stars was an Irish success story. Bred in Ireland, trained in Ireland, ridden by an Irishman and now retired to stud in Ireland, this horse was one-in-a-million. The frustrating element to flat racing is that once a fantastic three-year-old career ends, the horse is usually retired to breed. That's it. If you were lucky enough to watch Sea the Stars win the Arc, you'll know what I am talking about. If you haven't, even if you couldn't give a monkey's about nags – I urge you to get on to YouTube and watch that race. It would put hairs on the back of any neck. And because I knew he was a certainty, I didn't have even five cent on the animal. It's not always about money.

"Go. *Go!*" I urged the horse on the television screen. It was the year 2000. This was a day when the money was down. Of course the horse couldn't hear me, but nevertheless he responded to my cajoling with an imaginary whip, relentlessly wearing down the front runner in the last 2 furlongs. His effort took an aeon in my mind, but eventually he strode to the front and surged past the winning post in style. The horse's name was Sinndar, and he had just won the Epsom Derby.

I would judge the Arc as a close second, but the Epsom Derby is *the* race in the sport of flat racing. First run 221 years ago, it's the crown jewel in the sport's calendar. Restricted to three-year-olds, it's meant to be and often proves the ultimate test of equine speed and stamina. A Derby winner is a licence to print money for breeding.

If you want to make a profit on flat racing, it takes a lot of hard work and dedication, more so to my mind than the jumps. If you have a full-time job, that may be difficult, so we'll just touch on the big races which in my view attract the most interest from the sporting (and betting) public. They are the five 'Classics' for three-year-olds in Ireland and England, the Irish Champion Stakes, the King George VI and Queen Elizabeth Stakes at Ascot and the Prix de l'Arc de Triomphe.

National Hunt racing is easier to compartmentalise, because the focus is on the festivals i.e. Cheltenham, Aintree and Punchestown. In flat racing, the best horses are lightly campaigned between May and October, resulting in some very big races for the top horses, and some very big handicaps over a range of distances for colts and fillies at a lower level. Of course there are excellent meetings such as Royal Ascot and Derby weekend at the Curragh, but in general, you would want to have a firm grasp of flat form to be getting heavily involved as a punter, given the horses run so frequently and there are so many variables involved in weighing up a selection. The main areas of concern in betting on flat racing are the distance (some horses are best over 5 furlongs, others are suited to running over 8 furlongs i.e. 1 mile); breeding (because the margins are so small at the finish line, a horse's bloodline will be a key indicator of their best distance); the ground (some flat horses cannot handle soft ground, while others can punch above their weight on it); the track; and the draw.

Flat racing takes place from numbered stalls to ensure a level playing field – as we could be betting on a photo finish after the race. However, some tracks have a marked draw bias from the stalls that needs to be factored into your betting. For example, Chester is a very tight, turning track, so horses drawn low which have the benefit of the rail have a much better chance of winning in a 5-furlong sprint than their opponents drawn on the outside. A draw bias is not too dissimilar to a 200 metres race in athletics, where lanes one (on the inside) and eight (on the outside) are not the most advantageous. Rain or excessive watering of a track by a course to guarantee safe ground for the horses can also produce a draw bias, especially when there are thirty runners in a 6-furlong sprint and the jockeys decide to bunch into two groups at opposite sides of the course, searching for better ground to make their colt or filly run faster. The only way to get a handle on draw bias is to consult the trade publications such as the *Racing Post* and then watch the races before the one you wish to back. For example, the Lincoln handicap is run at Doncaster every year in March and the impact of the draw is generally illustrated by the previous day's racing. However, if a race is in excess of a mile, the draw has less impact, because the horses have to get into one pack and the jockeys must jostle for position.

Distance really is a big area for me when I study form for the flat. A horse that finishes well over 6 furlongs and is then declared to run over 7 furlongs will attract my attention, as will a horse that is moving down from 1 mile 2 furlongs to 1 mile after running out of gas over the longer trip.

Fitness is also relevant when backing flat horses, especially at the start of the campaign in April and May. A 3-year-old colt or filly may have a Group 1 target later in the summer, and the trainer may wish to bring him or her along slowly early in the season before pouncing on the key day. Fitness was to the fore when trainer Tommy Stack trained four winners at cumulative odds of 3,387/1 on the opening day of the Irish flat season at the Curragh in 2010. His horses were ready. On the other hand, 2009 Irish Derby winner Fame and Glory appeared for the first time in 2010 in a race at the Curragh in April and the horse was clearly not fit, fading into third at odds of 2/5. So you need to be careful. The same goes for handicaps. With big pots up for grabs and luck in-running part of the equation, some owners and trainers decide to aim for one big race in the summer and the horse's other races around that are secondary as they look to protect a handicap mark. A flat horse may consistently do well in handicap races without winning and then find life tough as it has to carry too much weight in subsequent races. The element of chance during a flat race can be a pain in the neck. You may have backed the best horse, but if his jockey has no room 2 furlongs out and cannot get a clear run, your money is gone. And then the darn thing may win the next time.

**The Derby** is where we begin our look at flat racing, because it's the most famous race of them all. Epsom is a difficult course for a horse to navigate, especially over the Derby distance of 1 mile 4 furlongs. The horses begin the race with an uphill climb for the first half mile so, for a jockey, getting a nice position is important, as it's not easy to weave through traffic at high speed on a twisting, undulating course. Then the horses begin to hurtle downhill, before rounding Tattenham Corner, a steep twist on the course. And then the race really catches fire as they go for home downhill before meeting the rising ground again at the finish. Many winners of the 2000 Guineas over 1 mile have been found out in the Derby through a lack of stamina, while other horses, with not many runs in their racing life at three, find the demands of the course impossible to handle.

**Workforce (6/1)** won the 2010 **Epsom Derby** in June, giving trainer Michael Stoute his fifth win in the race. The horse won at Goodwood as a two-year-old juvenile, proving he could handle a similarly undulating track, before finishing second behind Cape Blanco in the Dante Derby Trial over 10 furlongs at York. Workforce appeared inexperienced on that occasion, but finished well, indicating that his ability to stay the trip at Epsom was not in question. Workforce's dam (mother), was a sister to St Leger winner Brian Boru, so that was a positive for his chances of staying on breeding. Workforce became the first ever horse to be beaten in a Dante and win a Derby, but statistics are there to be broken. I wasn't a fan of this horse, but he proved me wrong by coming very well off a furious pace to win comfortably.

Generally, when we look for a Derby winner, we should concentrate on those in the first four in the betting as Workforce was, as each of the last ten Derby winners have come from the first four in the market. Between 1975 and 2010, only one horse (High-Rise in 1998) won at odds greater than 14/1. Also, the last horse not to finish either first or second on their last outing before the race was Dr Devious in 1992, proving that only in-form contenders need apply.

Middle-distance champions Montjeu and Galileo have sired, or fathered, Derby winners in recent years, so breeding must be noted.

Aidan O'Brien, John Oxx and Jim Bolger have done Ireland proud, winning five of the renewals since 2000, but there hasn't been a French-trained winner since 1976.

Since 2000, three horses have won the Dante Trial and another three horses have claimed the Derrinstown Stud Derby Trial at Leopardstown before winning at Epsom.

I have only ever tipped one Derby winner on air, when jockey Frankie Dettori, who had never won the race, broke his duck on 5/4 hot favourite Authorized in 2007. This horse won the Dante Trial at York easily in preparation, possessing what all Derby winners require, a turn of foot. Dettori had him in the right position coming down the hill and it was just a matter of the jockey pushing the button.

Apart from the Dancing Brave debacle in 1986, the best horse usually wins the Derby.

**Snow Fairy (9/1)** was the winner of the 2010 **Epsom Oaks** in June – and once again, this was a filly in form, as she became the seventh Oaks winner in ten years to win having also won on her most recent start. Snow Fairy's success was a bit of a fairy story, as she had cost only €1,800 as a yearling and raced six times as a juvenile, winning once. However, her form at three years of age was much improved and she put up a visually impressive display at Goodwood in May, travelling strongly before cruising to the front to win with ease. Similar tactics were deployed at Epsom, as her jockey Ryan Moore waited and waited before allowing her to unleash a devastating burst over the closing stages. In terms of class, Snow Fairy had a lot to find against the field, but her trainer Ed Dunlop had saddled the winner of the race before with Ouija Board, so he knew what he had on his hands.

In general terms, eight of the last ten Oaks winners came from the first five in the betting. Trainer Henry Cecil has an astounding record in this race, with eight winners in total to his name. Aidan O'Brien has also trained a couple of winners in the last decade and as the trip is the same as that of the Derby, the same rules count when it comes to breeding.

**Makfi (33/1)** took the first English Classic of the 2010 season, the **English 2000 Guineas** for colts over a mile at Newmarket in May. This French-trained horse was snubbed by wealthy owners as a juvenile, but he came into the race unbeaten and the manner of his victory confirmed him as a high-class thoroughbred. Makfi displayed a brilliant cruising speed and when his jockey Christophe Lemaire asked the question, the horse put the race to bed. That 2000 Guineas was all about the disappointing show of Aidan O'Brien's St Nicholas Abbey, who was rumoured to be the next Sea the Stars.

Unfortunately, a horse of Sea the Stars' ability is the exception rather than the rule and, being bred by the middle-distance champion Montjeu, St Nicholas Abbey found the mile too short. I certainly fell for the hype and the whispers, because I tipped him, but sometimes the facts are actually in front of your face. He never got to run at Epsom because of a muscle injury, so we'll never know if he was to become the three-year-old middle-distance king. Aidan O'Brien also sent out another hype horse, One Cool Cat, in 2004 and that highly strung beast couldn't cope with the day at all. To his credit, O'Brien has trained the winner of this race four times in the last decade, including two decent-priced winners in Rock of Gibraltar (9/1 in 2002) and Henrythenavigator (11/1 in 2008).

2004 winner Haafhd (11/2) had won over the course and distance before his victory, while Refuse to Bend, who landed the race for Dermot Weld in 2003, took a Leopardstown trial over the same distance as preparation. Wellbeing is therefore important in what is the first real test of these racehorses' lives. In 2009, Sea the Stars was the first horse in twenty years to win the Guineas and then go on to win the Epsom Derby, so you need to concentrate on specialist milers.

**Special Duty (9/2F)** took the **English 1000 Guineas** over a mile for fillies at Newmarket in the stewards' room, as the horse which beat her in a photo, Jacqueline Quest, interfered with Special Duty up the run-in. The rider of Jacqueline Quest, Tom Queally, didn't keep his horse straight and it cost him the race. The interesting thing about the French-trained Special Duty was that this champion two-year-old reappeared in France before the Guineas and was beaten over 7 furlongs on soft ground. A layer may have thought she would have stamina doubts, but her trainer, Criquette Head, was adamant in an interview before the race that she would stay. I wonder if she told Terence Trent D'Arby. I put Special Duty's run in France down to a lack of fitness, not stamina, so you must have all the information out there before backing or laying. It also rained at Newmarket that day, which had a serious impact on the draw. The horses at the stands-side rail gained a huge advantage and that is where Special Duty and Jacqueline Quest made their bids for glory. So glancing at the paper and ringing in a bet is not good enough when the TV experts tell you that there is a draw bias at the track on the day.

Fillies can take more time to come to themselves in comparison to colts, so the race has thrown up some mixed results over the past decade. Kazzia won on her British debut for Godolphin in 2002 at 14/1, while Russian Rhythm confounded strong vibes about her readiness by winning a year later at 12/1. 2009 winner Ghanaati was a 20/1 shot, who had prepared for the Guineas on an all-weather surface, while on the other hand, Finscéal Beo and Natagora, the winners in 2007 and 2008 respectively, went off at the top of the market after great juvenile campaigns. It's best not to go berserk in betting on the 1000 as a lot can happen in a filly's development between two and three and, unlike the Oaks, the trials are not as defining in estimating the chance of your choice.

**Arctic Cosmos (12/1)** was the winner of the **English St Leger**, the oldest of the Classics, at Doncaster in 2010. The St Leger doesn't have the sheen that it once did – the proximity of the Arc in Paris may have something to do with that – and in recent years, we have seen very few winners of any of the European Derbies even line up in the race. The race is run over 1 mile 6 furlongs, so you need a staying type and a lot of horses that run well in a Derby can appreciate the extra distance. Of late, Scorpion was second in an Irish Derby before winning a St Leger, Rule of Law was second at Epsom before going one better and Lucarno was fourth at Epsom in advance of his St Leger win. Another indicator of St Leger success is the Great Voltigeur Stakes, which takes place at the Ebor meeting in York in August. In fact, six of the last ten St Leger winners have finished in the first three at the Great Voltigeur. Arctic Cosmos didn't take that route, but he did finish second at Royal Ascot to Monterosso, a horse who would go off favourite for the Irish Derby. An in-form stable, the application of blinkers, and a decent ride close to the pace by pilot William Buick enabled Arctic Cosmos to take a lead which he never surrendered. As I indicated, the St Leger is not the crème de la crème these days, so that can bring the less classy types into your calculations. Concentrate on those that will stay. One thing in favour of Arctic Cosmos was that he had finished in the top three on his last start, which every St Leger winner has done for the last ten years. In terms of trainer trends, Aidan O'Brien has taken the race three times in the last ten years, while Godolphin's Saeed bin Suroor has sent out the winner five times since 1995.

**Harbinger (4/1)** was the runaway winner of the **King George VI and Queen Elizabeth Stakes at Ascot,** which is something his owners can savour as he suffered a leg fracture on the gallops afterwards, prompting immediate retirement. Harbinger had a truncated three-year-old campaign, before improving at the rate of knots with wins at Newbury, Chester and Royal Ascot in 2010. In what I would describe as a muddling race, despite the fast time, Harbinger picked off two Derby winners, Workforce and Cape Blanco, like flies. As they say in racing, 'he bolted up'. Never discount the rate of improvement a horse can make – such an improvement made Harbinger the best-rated horse in the world for a brief time. Harbinger was a four-year-old, so he had the age advantage over the younger pretenders, and that can be important in this race. In fact, Alamshar and Galileo are the only three-year-olds to have won in the past decade, but it is worth noting that a lot of the best three-year-olds, such as Sea the Stars in 2009 and Motivator in 2005, ran in the Eclipse Stakes at Sandown. Trainer Michael Stoute has won the last two renewals and before him Aidan O'Brien made it two on the bounce, but I would take the view that it's merely a reflection of their dominance in the sport. Before

Harbinger, the previous six winners went off favourite, so don't be backing 33/1 shots.

Time to look closer to home, and the **2010 Irish Derby** at the **Curragh** was won by **Cape Blanco (7/2)**. This, you may remember, was the horse which beat Epsom winner Workforce at York. He then flopped in the French Derby, but every horse can have an off day, especially if they have to travel abroad. Cape Blanco was the choice of Ballydoyle's then stable jockey Johnny Murtagh, which didn't mean he was on the right one, but in this instance, he was. Cape Blanco is a son of former Epsom and Irish Derby winner Galileo, so his ability at the trip was never in question. The Irish Derby suffers in that it is held after the Epsom equivalent, so many English horses bypass it for events at home.

The Curragh, which hosts all five Irish Classics, is a straightforward right-handed track. It's more or less flat and, when they hold the Derby, it's a straight run from 4 furlongs out. Cape Blanco was part of a 1-2-3 in 2010 for Aidan O'Brien, who has won the race for the last five years. So he's your starting point. It does pay to keep an eye on his second or even third string (not the stable's fancied horse), as Frozen Fire won in 2008 at 16/1 and Soldier of Fortune took advantage of the prevailing soft conditions to win at odds of 5/1 in 2007. Two horses that have finished third at Epsom, Dylan Thomas (2006) and Alamshar (2003), have gone to the Curragh and won. North Light was the last Epsom Derby winner to try his luck in 2004 and he was beaten by 10/1 shot Grey Swallow. However, Sinndar, Galileo and High Chaparral were easy winners when they did the Epsom-Curragh double at the beginning of the millennium. There hasn't been a winner of the race trained in England since Balanchine in 1994.

The 2010 **Irish Oaks** was won by Snow Fairy, who was a fantastic price at 3/1 considering her Epsom exploits. And her jockey Ryan Moore gave her another hold-up ride before picking off the leaders and taking the prize comfortably. This is the race in which I backed the horse which finished third, Lady Lupus, at 200/1 each way on the Friday, knowing from a stable tour that Aidan O'Brien's son, Joseph, was schooling top horses down at Ballydoyle and could be in line to ride in a big race. Snow Fairy's trainer, Ed Dunlop, also brought Ouija Board and Lailani to win our Oaks, so unlike the Irish Derby, English trainers do have success at the Curragh, with six away victories since 1999. The race is held later than the Irish Derby, giving English horses more time to recover from the Epsom Oaks. O'Brien saddled a hat-trick of winners in the race between 2006 and 2008 at short odds, but his Quarter Moon was turned over by 33/1 outsider Margarula in 2002. Vintage Tipple, a 12/1 chance, won for the late great Paddy Mullins a year later, so shocks are not out of the question. In addition to Snow Fairy; Alexandrova, Ouija Board and Sariska have completed the Epsom-Curragh double in recent years, so I wouldn't lay an Epsom winner.

**Canford Cliffs (9/4F)** was one of the easiest **Irish 2000 Guineas** winners I have seen, and it was not surprising after his solid performance in finishing third at Newmarket. His trainer, Richard Hannon, won the race in 1987 and 1990 at the Curragh. Canford Cliffs was the sixth English winner in the last decade. He also became the ninth successive winner of the Irish 2000 to appear after running at Newmarket. With some horses, such as Rock of Gibraltar, Henrythenavigator and Cockney Rebel, the English-Irish double was landed, but others showed dramatic improvement. Softer ground aided 2003 winner Indian Haven and the same statement can be applied to 2006 winner Araafa, so remember that ground can have a huge say in the destination of the top prizes over these short distances. 2001 winner Black Minnaloushe was a 20/1 surprise for Aidan O'Brien, which is another reason to forensically examine all of his runners. Unless he has entered a confirmed pacemaker, consider them all.

**Bethrah (16/1)** was the surprise winner of the **Irish 1000 Guineas**, giving trainer Dermot Weld his second success in five years. In 2006, he sent out 12/1 winner Nightime, so his runners must be noted. All of the last ten winners had won over at least 7 furlongs and, in Bethrah's case, she won a trial at Leopardstown. There have been some short-priced winners – Newmarket champions Finscéal Beo and Attraction turned up for more oats at the Curragh – but once again Aidan O'Brien has saddled a couple of 'second string' winners.

Imagine was a 16/1 winner for O'Brien in 2001 and then Halfway to Heaven won at odds of 13/2 in 2008. I backed Music Show in 2010 and she finished third, before winning at 13/2 in a weaker race at Newmarket. That's why the flat can be like a bluebottle in a room.

The **Irish St Leger** is quite a straightforward race to analyse. Over the same trip as its English equivalent, the difference is that it allows horses older than three to contest for the honours, and this has meant no three-year-old has won since the Dermot Weld trained Vinnie Roe in 2001. Vinnie Roe was a St Leger specialist, winning four times on the bounce, so you could argue that he won in '01 in spite of his age. Vintage Crop, Oscar Schindler and Kayf Tara have also won the race more than once, so you can read into that what you will. The 2010 winner Sans Frontieres was backed in the morning, went off at 11/8, and was the highest-rated horse in the field. His jockey Olivier Peslier gave him a fantastic ride, judging the pace of the race perfectly. Sans Frontieres was the tenth successive winner to have finished either first or second on his previous run. Aidan O'Brien didn't train the winner of this race until 2007. John Oxx has trained two winners in the last five years, so his runners merit an eye or two.

The running of the 2001 **Champion Stakes** at **Leopardstown** was one of the best flat races I have ever seen. Fantastic Light's defeat of Galileo in a thrilling finish elevated the Group 1 contest over 10 furlongs in my mind. Increased prize money and the eligibility of the winner to line up at the Breeders Cup in America have been carrots, so the race tends to attract the best on offer. Sea the Stars won this in 2009, becoming the third successive odds-on shot to win. That makes the 6/1 victory of Cape Blanco in 2010 a refreshing change. It also highlights yet again why Aidan O'Brien's horses always run on their merits when they are fully wound up and that the stable jockey may not always be right. On this occasion, Johnny Murtagh was on the wrong one and Seamus Heffernan stole a lead on his rivals. Heffernan's tactics were spot on and they couldn't catch the Irish Derby winner. The presence of the four-year-old, Rip Van Winkle, certainly made Cape Blanco an attractive price and Heffernan rewarded backers with an exceptional steer, exposing the field's stamina on rain-softened ground.

For layers, note that the last ten winners of this race all had victories at Group 1 level. Also, three-year-olds have a decent recent record, with Epsom Derby winners New Approach and Sea the Stars following up, while I cannot understand why 2005 Sandown Eclipse winner Oratorio went off at 7/1 to win over the same distance later in the season, following his 12/1 victory over Epsom Derby winner Motivator that summer.

Finally, in our dissection of the best flat races, we come to the **Prix de l'Arc de Triomphe**, which is in effect the European Championship, **at Longchamp** in October. This is the arena where the best three-year-olds compete against their elders over a mile and a half. Longchamp, like the Curragh, is right-handed, flat, and turning. Workforce added to his Derby success by winning the 2010 Arc at odds of 6/1, the same price at which he won the Derby. The softer ground didn't inconvenience him and from watching it again, I feel big fields suited Workforce, who is a mercurial type of colt. He needed things to fall his way, which they did in the Derby and again in the Arc, as the race was set up for him to announce his presence. Why Ryan Moore has been champion jockey in the UK and is employed by Michael Stoute was as clear as day in this one, as he gave every sinew of his being on Workforce in the last 100 yards, while the challenger, Nakayama Festa, had a statue on board. And that was the difference between victory and defeat.

Unlike the King George, three-year-olds have dominated the Arc, with fourteen of the last seventeen runnings going to a three-year-old. Forget about five-year-olds as there have only been two five-year-old winners in the past thirty-five years.

There are some other pertinent trends. Fourteen of the last seventeen Arc winners were in stall seven or lower. Trainer John Oxx has won the race more times than Aidan O'Brien, but French trainer André Fabre has trained the winner seven times in the last quarter of a century. Workforce and Sea the Stars have done wonders for Epsom Derby form in recent years, but scratch the surface and you will notice that Authorized, Motivator, North Light, Kris Kin and High-Rise all flopped in the

Arc. Recently, the French preparatory race, the Prix
Niel, over the same course and distance, has provided
an excellent guide, with Sinndar, Dalakhani, Hurricane
Run and Rail Link all winning it before going on to
claim the Arc. 2004 winner Bago was the biggest priced
winner at 10/1 in recent times, so I'd stick to the fancied
types when making your *choix*.

# Chapter 10

*The Majors*

## The Masters

I missed the moment. The moment I had been waiting for. I had been waiting for years. I first noticed Phil Mickelson at the 1996 US Masters, when he led early and finished third. I would regularly back him because I thought he was a major winner in waiting. He was a great putter, imaginative around the greens, accurate with his irons and, above all, aggressive. He made golf fun to watch, as you could strap yourself into the couch and look forward to the rollercoaster, the brilliance, the recovery shots followed by a dollop of stupidity. It was a no-brainer for me, with his talent, that Mickelson would win a major golf championship, but it took a lot longer than I expected. I backed him in the 2001 Masters and he lost out to Tiger Woods on the Sunday, missing short putts at crucial stages. I backed him in the 2001 US PGA Championship in Atlanta, and he went down by a shot to David Toms. It was becoming frustrating. I then backed him in the 2002 US Open in New York and he finished second to Woods. His 2003 performances were below par, but when you follow a player closely, you get a sense of when it is their time. I read a lot about golf, trying to detect good information which will decide my financial involvement. Mickelson had become serious about his weight and engaged short-game guru Dave Pelz before the 2004 season. He had worked on shortening his distance from the tee and finding more fairways. He was curbing the gung-ho philosophy and becoming smarter. It was necessary, because his performance in the 2003 Presidents Cup had been hopeless. The biggest lesson I learned from Mickelson, and his first major win at the 2004 Masters, was that natural talent could dig a sportsperson out of any slump. I noticed that things were different when he won the 2004 Bob Hope Classic, a regular tournament at the start of the season. His aura was calm and confident. It was going to be a breakthrough season, which in Mickelson's case meant a major. I knew it instinctively. Mickelson drove up Magnolia Lane at Augusta for the 2004 Masters with a hat trick of third-place finishes in the tournament in the previous three years. I was certain and conveyed such sentiments to Ian Dempsey on the Thursday morning. I missed the 33/1 available in January. Mickelson was 9/1 on the week of the event. Still, with Tiger Woods coming off the back of swing changes, it was not a bad price. In the final round, Mickelson, who was tied for the lead on the Saturday night, stumbled early, dropping back to 4 under par and leaving the door open for Ernie Els to surge to 8 under by the time he had completed his round. Mickelson then went and birdied 12, 13, 14 and 16 to draw level with Els going down the last hole, his 72nd hole.

I was reading the midnight sports bulletin on TODAY FM. I thought to myself, "Great, a play off! We have a chance!" Mickelson hit his second shot to 20 feet on the 18th and I went into the studio, telling the listeners that it was looking like a play-off between Mickelson and Els, two players who had battled it out for the 1984 World Junior Championship as fourteen-year-olds. When I came out from the studio, Mickelson was hugging his children. "What?" It took me about a minute to realise that he had actually won the Masters. Unlike Phil, I had missed the winning putt. The texts and calls soon flowed. It was strange. People knew how much I had talked about Phil Mickelson and believed in him. People were contacting me because this tournament penetrates the masses. They were interested in Phil's story too. And that interest in a big event is one of the reasons why Augusta is marked in luminous pen on our sporting calendar.

Phil Mickelson (14/1); Lee Westwood (24/1); Anthony Kim (40/1); Tiger Woods (6/1); and KJ Choi (85/1). If you know your golf, and you saw those five names, and if you were told they filled the top five places at the 2010 US Masters Tournament, then you would probably not be too surprised. For me, the Masters at Augusta National is the easiest of the four annual major golf championships to analyse for contenders. Sports junkies love the Masters. It's regularly held on the same weekend as the Aintree Grand National in early April, and for me, it's always signified the start of a sporting summer. My first memory of the Masters was watching Larry Mize chipping in to win the green jacket in 1987. Many sports fans have been captivated by Jack Nicklaus, Seve Ballesteros, Nick Faldo and Tiger Woods painting the pictures of sporting history on this beautifully manicured golf course in Georgia in the south-eastern part of the United States.

The tournament has taken on a magisterial air since the great amateur Bobby Jones helped establish it back in the 1930s. At Augusta, the azaleas are in full bloom and every blade of grass is a little greener than anywhere else. The holes are etched in my mind. The tough par 4 11th hole, the 12th hole – a par 3 over water, and the 13th – a long par 5. These holes constitute what they call Amen Corner. The ceremonial aspects of the Masters portray its unique appeal: the presentation of a green jacket to the winner; the lack of on-course advertising; the Champions' dinner exclusively for tournament winners. For years, as a spectacle, the Masters has been a risk and reward affair, with water coming into play down the closing stretch of holes, often producing extraordinary TV moments. See Tiger Woods, 16th hole, final round, 2005.

So how do we pick a Master? 1979 is a long time ago, and that's the last time a rookie, or a debutant, won the Masters. Fuzzy Zoeller was that rookie, and he had little time to think about the magnitude of his achievement as he won in the most unlikely of play-offs after Ed Sneed suffered a golfing meltdown on the closing holes. The point here is that experience is everything when making your picks for the Masters. It's an incredible test of golf, and players, even at the elite level, need to find their bearings over a couple of visits before they can be classified as realistic contenders. 2010 winner Phil Mickelson was chasing his third green jacket after wins in 2004 and 2006, so he was an obvious challenger at 14/1. Experience has made current champion Phil Mickelson into the formidable player that he is at Augusta. His record at the Masters is simply incredible. Between 1995 and 2010, he finished in the Top 10 thirteen times from sixteen attempts. So write down the letter 'E' for experience.

Putting is the element that ranks second only to experience when ranking the Masters field. Tiger Woods has won four green jackets, and he's the best clutch putter under pressure around. Augusta National's teeth are its lightning quick greens, with treacherous breaks and slopes. It's what they call a 'second shot course' where the punishment for a stray tee shot is not as severe as at the US Open. A player can manage his ball from the rough at Augusta, but the key to winning is to land iron shots in the right areas of the greens with a high ball flight. Then the player needs to make the putts. The ability to chip well around the greens is also necessary. Colin Montgomerie had a fantastic game in his prime from tee to green, but his putting has always been inconsistent and that's reflected in his poor Masters record. Lee Trevino had a low ball flight and couldn't handle the course. On the other hand, Seve Ballesteros was a genius with the putter, and he had plenty of opportunities to add to his Masters victories of 1980 and 1983. The 1984 and 1995 winner, Ben Crenshaw, was one of the best ever players with what they call the 'Texas Wedge' (a nickname for a putter). José Maria Olazábal, who won in 1994 and 1999, was one of the best iron and short game players to emerge from Europe. 2003 champion Mike Weir was another natural putter, who had a tendency to win tournaments when in contention.

That brings us to another word beginning with the letter 'P': pressure. Jumps jockey Barry Geraghty once said that pressure was for tyres and he's won all of the big UK races. Major championship golf is a very individual and mental pursuit, and when a golfer is trying to repeat the same shot again and again, it's easy to become distracted by the thought of what could be achieved. Some players just can't handle it. In recent years I have watched Len Mattiace and Brandt Snedeker break down in tears after blowing their chance to win the Masters. Kenny Perry had a great chance to win in 2009, but couldn't handle the pressure. And believe me, he'll never win a major on the regular tour. Greg Norman provided the ultimate example of choking, or losing control, at the Masters. It is why sport brings a tragic element – it's what makes us enthralled as bystanders. Norman lost that first Masters I watched to

Mize and he was desperately unlucky, as Mize holed that chip from off the green in a play-off, turning a probable loss into a major title. A year previously, Norman lost out to fate in the form of 46-year-old Jack Nicklaus shooting 65 to win his sixth green jacket. Ten years later, in 1996, it looked as if it was finally Norman's time. He took a six-shot lead over Nick Faldo into the final round. He was playing perfect golf and couldn't lose. It was impossible to lose. And then we witnessed one of the greatest collapses in sporting history, as Faldo shot 67 and Norman took 78, his hopes disintegrating over four hours. What it means from a betting perspective is that we can analyse past results and put a line through certain players, while having others on our side. I don't believe Ernie Els, now in his forties, will ever win the Masters, because I think he wants to win it too much. I also don't think Padraig Harrington will ever win at Augusta, because from observing his interviews he is too cerebral about it being the ultimate test. Harrington is our greatest living sportsman, but he went around the practice rounds in 2010 with a spirit level. I felt that was the territory of information overload. Harrington went and missed the cut. The question I always ask come Major time, a question I don't ask as regularly for US PGA Tour betting is: *"Is the laddie in control of his emotions?"* That's not a quote for the ages, just a voice in my head with a Scottish brogue.

There was a three-year-period from 2007 to 2009 when the Masters was a little out of sync for the consistent punter. Zach Johnson, Trevor Immelman and Angel Cabrera won the tournament, as the organisers let a little bit of air out of the fun balloon, narrowing fairways and penalising tee shots more than usual. It became in my mind a carbon copy of the US Open. It led to a winning score of 1 over par for Johnson, only ten players under par in Immelman's year and three surprise names in the play-off when Cabrera won (Perry and Chad Campbell were the others). Thankfully normal service was resumed with a fair test in 2010 and Mickelson came home with a 16 under par total. So when you are faced with a changing course, be careful from a betting perspective. It pays to listen to what the players say about the course in the practice rounds. If they are grumbling, they are already making mental bogeys.

Johnson was a shock winner in 2007 at 200/1, but this dude was a prolific winner on the Nationwide Tour, the secondary US golf tour, so he knew how to close the sale. He also has a great iron game and a solid putting stroke, highlighted by his second place finish at the Memorial Tournament in 2006, at the Muirfield Village course designed by Jack Nicklaus and similar to Augusta in the challenges posed. Johnson also made the American Ryder Cup team that year which left Ireland humiliated after Europe took them apart at the K Club. The point is that Johnson was one of America's best golfers. A major win for the Iowan was a possibility. Immelman had a fifth place finish at the 2005 Masters, therefore his ability to conquer Augusta in 2008 was not in question. An excellent CV on the European Tour (he had won three times before the age of thirty) was buttressed by a winning move to the US Tour when he took the Western Open in 2006. So he wasn't a stunning winner at 150/1, but what was surprising was that he carried no form into Augusta on the week of his victory. Cabrera has only won two tournaments in America – the 2007 US Open and the 2009 Masters. He's also won the European Tour's flagship event, the PGA Championship in just three victories on this side of the pond. So it's probably fair to say that the Argentine has a book at home on the economies of scale, or has a crystal ball and is picking his victories in advance. Cabrera, who was a 140/1 shot when he won, had three Top 10 finishes at the Masters before he won that play-off. The problem is that he's always been a difficult player to get a handle on – he smokes drive after drive and sinks the putts when in the mood – but when he's woken up on the wrong side of the bed he makes silly mistakes. You should never discount a previous major winner at Augusta, so I believe it was a lot easier for Cabrera to win in the knowledge that he had already completed the job at Oakmont in the US Open.

When I look back on my tips for the 2010 Masters, I see the names Paul Casey, Dustin Johnson, Luke Donald and Ryan Moore. None of them contended. Casey was saving his performance for the British Open. Johnson wasn't that bad a selection given his displays at the US Open and the US PGA later in the year. Donald is Donald and I don't know why I tipped him. He flatters to deceive. Moore topped the putting statistics for the week but the rest of his game was at a C level. So I was going to lose money, right? Wrong. In-running betting is important in golf because by watching the action unfold you can sense what may happen on the back nine holes on Sunday. At halfway, I had made my mind up on two things. Mickelson, who started the week at a decent price after some indifferent form, was very happy with his game and said as much in an interview on the Friday evening. To see Mickelson radiate such confidence about his game made 11/2 on the American a very good each-way bet, as he was only two shots behind Lee Westwood and Ian Poulter at halfway. I didn't act on it, as I prefer to cut my losses on a win market and not throw potentially good money after bad. However, on the lay side of things, I got involved, and as I have mentioned in an earlier chapter, I took a bet on Woods to even up my book for the tournament. Sunday was all about Westwood and Mickelson and it was clear early on that Westwood couldn't buy a putt. On the contrary, Mickelson was able to extract himself from difficult lies, salvage par, make a birdie at the 12th and then win the tournament with some artistic brilliance on the 13th. On that hole he took on the water with his second shot from the pine straw around the trees and carded a birdie. The difference between a major champion, Mickelson, and a major contender,

Westwood, was pretty stark from my armchair. Mickelson ended up winning by three shots.

## The US Open

Graeme McDowell, huh? Yep. Golden Graeme Cracker. Yep. 80/1. Easy. Yep. Eh, no. The US Open is the second major of the year, held every June, and it's a tricky tournament to predict. It's a double-edged sword in that it's hard to find the winner, but you can have a crack at big-priced players each way to attempt the acquisition of profit. I have tipped the winner on the radio once and that was in 2003, when Jim Furyk won at odds of 33/1, as already mentioned. The US Open has traditionally been a brutal test, with the United States Golf Association guided by the principle that par is sacred, and the winning score should be around par. Unlike the Masters, the US Open is played on various courses, not a rota *per se*, but there's usually a gap of a significant number of years for the event to return to a particular course.

When I look at my own historical bets for the US Open that are not named Jim Furyk, I have found that I'm either on the money or very wrong. In 2002, I backed Phil Mickelson. The course, Bethpage Black, was a bomber's track, where big hitters would have a major advantage, so I felt that would suit Phil. He finished second. I had money on Jeff Maggert each way at 150/1 in 2004. That was a confident pick despite the price, as he'd tied 4th at the course, Shinnecock Hills, in 1995 and rattled off three successive Top 10s in the US Open between 1997 and 1999, before placing third in 2002. At Shinnecock Hills in 2004, Maggert was third again, giving a return on the place side of the bet of 37½ to 1. So a decent historical record in the event does not hold as much weight as in the Masters, but it does matter, as the USGA sets up its courses a certain way. I backed Padraig Harrington in 2006 at Winged Foot and we'll talk about that later.

When we look at the winners of the US Open since 2005, five of the last six of them have been first-time major winners. Michael Campbell, a 200/1 nobody as far as the layers were concerned in 2005, had to qualify to get to Pinehurst. Before his triumph he had never won in America. He did nearly win the Open at St Andrews in 1995, but I only know one person on the planet who backed Michael Campbell that week. And it wasn't me. The 2006 winner, Geoff Ogilvy, had only won twice on the US PGA Tour before his unexpected 100/1 success. This was a result of Ogilvy's gritty play down the stretch (a chip-in on 17, a good par save on 18) and the monumental collapse of two players: Phil Mickelson, who made double bogey from 4 over par on the last by driving it into oblivion; and upsettingly for any fan of the game, Colin Montgomerie, who reached the fairway on 4 over on the 18th and then buried his approach into the Vietnam jungle, also making double. 2007 was about 150/1 shot Angel Cabrera getting into a rhythm, finishing early – and watching Tiger Woods and Jim Furyk falter. 2008 was about Woods (a 7/2 chance) winning on one leg at Torrey Pines, a course which he had owned on the regular tour at the Buick Invitational, now known as the Farmers Insurance Open.

The 2009 US Open was a personal disaster for me, but not for a man called John from Knocklyon in Dublin. This is my biggest betting regret, period. Lucas Glover was a player I'd always kept an eye on, because he started on the US PGA Tour playing tough golf courses like Quail Hollow well and eventually he won a tournament called the Walt Disney Classic in Florida in 2005. I kid you not. I liked Lucas' long game, so I tipped him at the Houston Open before the 2009 Masters, and the moment he grabbed a share of the lead, the palpitations began and he went double, triple, triple bogey. Maybe he wanted ice cream. Come the US Open at Bethpage Black, a course I knew would suit him, I was all about tipping Lucas to be the leader after the first round at 125/1. The outright market covers the four rounds, but the first round market only covers day one. Unbeknownst to me, a seasoned American golf journalist called Bob Bubka had tipped Glover outright on *Newstalk Radio* on the Wednesday night. Ian Dempsey then surprised me by asking about Glover on the Thursday. I chortled and assured Dempsey that Glover would freak out on the Sunday. So I went ahead and tipped him for first round leader and flagged three other outright bets for the audience. What happens? Ole Lucas is the second round leader and goes on to win the tournament at 225/1. I was being too clever by half, and should have had some money in the outright market. Glover was helped by rain delays which led to a Monday finish and took some of the major championship feel out of the event. He was also assisted by his golf game, which was stupendous all week and a resolve I didn't think he had. John from Knocklyon heard my tip and decided to back Glover outright. He texted in afterwards to mention he had just paid for a new kitchen.

I've never doubted the courage of a player such as Graeme McDowell – a Ryder Cup star who was a top college golfer in the US and won the Scandinavian Masters on his first season on the European Tour. Missing out on the 2006 Ryder Cup would have hurt McDowell, so it's always important to watch how somebody handles adversity, because if they can, they can come back twice as good and land you a big payday if you keep the faith. "Are you listening, Sergio Garcia?" McDowell changed his agent and got a new caddie and the results have followed. He kept his place in the Top 50 in the world ahead of the Wales Open, which meant he was exempt for the US Open at Pebble Beach. That confidence boost carried over into Wales, where he won at 22/1 by demolishing the Celtic Manor course. And we all know what happened later in the year at Celtic Manor. When I looked at McDowell ahead of Pebble, and yes, I did look – the cons outweighed the pros. The cons were a lack of Top 10 major championship finishes, the absence of a tournament win in America, the difficulty for anyone in putting back-to-back wins together, the pressure . . . The pros were his recent form, the course, which I believed would suit him, as windy conditions were no stranger to a man from Portrush, and a reasonably decent US Open record. An each-way bet on McDowell would be a bet with a sporting chance. The place part could give you a return, with a win a significant bonus. It wasn't Jim Furyk in 2003 by any means. The key is that we didn't know what McDowell was made of until he was the last man standing against bigger names such as Woods, Mickelson, and Ernie Els. Now it has happened, McDowell can certainly win more majors. The foil – or the choker – of this event was Dustin Johnson, who entered the final round with a three-shot lead and then shot 82, or 12 over par. It was a performance Vincent Price would have been proud of, which shows that for every Graeme McDowell, there is a Dustin Johnson. My headline tip for the 2010 US Open was Camilo Villegas, who carded a dreadful 78 in the opening round. Your selection can often lose the tournament on the first day. Villegas was never going to recover from that.

The US Open is what gambling should be. All about patience, patience, patience. Make par, make par, make par. McDowell finished on par. So look for gentlemen with a steady disposition and if recent years are anything to go by, try and find a competitor who has the potential to break through to the next level. The amount of big-priced winners at the US Open should tell you that a 200/1 chance is not a no-hoper. It may be in celebrity betting, but not in golf betting. 200/1 is 50/1 for a place, which is better than any horse race or football match. Gregory Havret was second to McDowell at Pebble Beach at 750/1! This is a man nobody backed, but he was a European Tour winner at Loch Lomond. So if you spot someone with good reason, forget about the price and go for it.

One more thing about the US Open. You should keep an eye out for repeat winners. Tiger Woods has won three times. Retief Goosen was 40/1 when he won for the second time in 2004. Ernie Els, Payne Stewart and Lee Janzen all won twice in the 1990s. Andy North won two US Opens and only one other PGA Tour event. Curtis Strange won two US Opens and they were his only majors. Hale Irwin won three US Opens and they were his only majors.

Looking ahead, the 2011 US Open will be held at Congressional Country Club in Maryland. It was last staged there in 1997, when Ernie Els edged out Colin Montgomerie to win. In recent years, Congressional has hosted the AT & T National tournament on the US PGA Tour. Tiger Woods won the event in 2009, Anthony Kim took the prize in 2008 and KJ Choi came home in front in 2007. Also, a different tournament, the Booz Allen Classic, was held at Congressional in 2005 and was won by Sergio Garcia. Of the non-winners, Jim Furyk, Adam Scott, Stuart Appleby, Robert Allenby, Ben Crane, Hunter Mahan and Brandt Snedeker have all performed well at Congressional, so check who is playing well in June. In 2012, the US Open will be held at the Olympic Club in San Francisco, which held the 1998 tournament, won by Lee Janzen.

## The Open

"Has he won yet, Tom?"

"Has he won?"

Thirty minutes elapse.

"What's happening?"

"Who?"

"What hole is he on?"

I made the relentless calls from Croke Park. I was on business, but my mind was on David Duval. It was 2001 and I was a cub of a punter. I had enough sense to realise that Duval, at 25/1, was the bargain of the century (they always are at the time) for the Open at Royal Lytham. He won comfortably, but I couldn't tell without a TV screen for company. The Floridian had been the world number one in 1999, was second in the 2001 Masters – and was the only player to have threatened Tiger Woods in the previous year's Open at St Andrews before disappearing into the Road Hole bunker, never to be seen again. Well, for a while anyway. That was back in the days when bookmakers were not clued in about golf odds.

A year later I backed Ernie Els at Muirfield at 16/1. That was another confident bet. Ernie had finished fifth as a wee boy at the course in 1992 and was one of the top players in the world, with two major titles in his garage.

It's time to examine golf's oldest major championship, The Open Championship or 'The British Open', as many describe it overseas. Padraig Harrington was voted Ireland's greatest ever sports person in a recent television programme and he is worthy of such recognition. The only time I have tipped the winner of the Open on-air was in 2007, when Harrington won at Carnoustie. Matt Cooper, TODAY FM's presenter of *The Last Word* and one of Ireland's leading journalists, was guesting on the *Breakfast Show* the week before. When I gave the tip, he gently mocked my selection of Harrington at 22/1. "But Harrington has never won a major," he said, questioning my belief that this was the Dubliner's time.

I had decided that it *was* Harrington's time from watching him over the previous year. He had made a clever move to play the Irish PGA on a links course at the European Club in Wicklow the week before Carnoustie and he won. Buoyed by a profitable World Cup, I stuck a bit each way on him at 66/1 in the 2006 US Open at Winged Foot. It struck me as one of those courses of beautiful brutality that Harrington would love, grinding out pars with his world-class short game. Harrington played an incredible final round and when he birdied the 14th hole to move into a share of the lead, I started pacing around the room with my hands around my back, like a school teacher waffling away at the class on a Tuesday afternoon in January. I began to mumble incoherently as the dollars (they are always dollars) flashed through my mind. It wasn't Flesch Redux – I had gone each way – it was the rewarding of my conviction at backing Harrington at 66/1 that made me nervous. It was not about the potential reward. It was about my belief in a fellow Dubliner who was chasing a first major title. Anyway, Harrington bogeyed the last three holes. He unravelled.

And then it happened again on the 18th hole of the 2007 Open at Carnoustie. Harrington lost his focus again with the winner's Claret Jug in his grasp. Not everyone shares that view, but it's what I believe. Until the 18th hole, Harrington had got into some type of zone from another planet. He certainly didn't look human as he made pars and a birdie down the back nine, with an eagle tucked in for good measure. I was imitating a rower on the sofa, leaning back and forth without the equipment or the exercise. This was a great Irish sports story in the making, an Eamonn Coghlan for our times. I didn't back Harrington because he was Irish, but his potential achievement, sixty years on from Fred Daly, was magnifying the tension, both for him, and for us. Harrington was one ahead on the 18th. We'd already seen Andrés Romero wilt under the searing heat of major pressure, and it was Harrington's to lose. In the back of my mind, I had known that Harrington lost in the semi-finals of the 1992 British Amateur by hitting the ball out of bounds on the 18th at Carnoustie, one of the toughest holes in golf, with the

Barry Burn dissecting the fairway. "Find the effing fairway!" I told the television. Then Harrington's drive struck the bridge and plopped into the water. "Aaaaaagh!" I moaned, head in hands, with half of Ireland's sports fans probably engaged in the same simultaneous reaction. I didn't have a split screen to watch them though. When Harrington belted his third shot into the water again, my reaction was more of resignation. He'd completely blown it. Harrington, though, is a resolute individual. He got up and down for a double bogey six, and when Sergio Garcia came down the 18th and took a bogey to allow Harrington back into the play-off, I knew he'd win it. Harrington was ready to win that major. He'd become one of the world's best golfers and he just needed a bit of luck. As punters, all we can do is hope, we can't expect. Harrington got his second chance, and he took it. He learned, and his subsequent wins in the 2008 Open and US PGA showed that he was able to perfect the art of winning major championships.

You see, that's the key. There's a lot of guessing involved in betting. Manchester United had to learn how to play football in Europe in the 1990s before they won the Champions League in 1999. Sometimes the breakthrough comes, even to the surprise of the individual who has broken through. I bet Louis Oosthuizen hoped, but may not have believed he would win a major championship when he teed it up for the 2010 Open at St Andrews. The twenty-seven-year-old was a 250/1 outsider, based on the fact that he'd only made one cut in eight major attempts. He wasn't remotely on the radar, and bar a very select few who lobbed small amounts on him in the win market at 500/1 on Betfair, nobody backed him. Oosthuizen had bits and pieces going for him. He was a recent winner on the European Tour and he'd performed well in 2010. The fairways of St Andrews were generous and this South African was used to 'European Tour' style greens, which are slower than the glass tables which are prevalent in America. What Oosthuizen did well was to take advantage of his tremendous break, in that he got the best of the conditions in the opening couple of days, and then kept his emotions in equilibrium over the weekend. What we saw from his challengers was a complete lack of mental discipline. Rory McIlroy shot a course record 63 on the first day and then lost his marbles by carding an 80 in a gale on the second day. He let the windy conditions affect him, and instead of grinding away, taking 75 shots and keeping himself in the tournament, he lost it on the Friday. The Ulsterman battled back brilliantly on the weekend to finish in a tie for third. It was just his inexperience that got in the way. A brittle mentality also sunk Paul Casey's challenge. He started the final round three shots behind Oosthuizen, but I wondered about his ability to put pressure on his opponent. I had seen too many missed putts and loose shots all week and all year to mark Casey out as the winner. I had tipped Casey in the Masters. He made triple bogey in his opening round and never recovered. I tipped him in the Players Championship. No. He made a triple bogey at the US Open. He made another one in the Open on the Friday. It was the clearest evidence that I had learned from my mistakes that I avoided touching Casey with a barge pole at the Open.

I have bought the *Racing Post* for many years, and my favourite ever headline came the day after the unknown American, Ben Curtis, won the Open at Royal St George's in 2003. '*The Ultimate Skinner*' was above a picture of Curtis. A skinner is when a bookmaker has a clean book on a competitor – i.e. no liability. Curtis was available at 750/1 before the tournament. No bookmakers took any money before Thursday's play on the rookie, who had posted a best finish of 13th in the Western Open on the PGA Tour before crossing the Atlantic. Only £87 was matched on Curtis at 999/1 on Betfair and I'm sure this was for trading purposes.

The Open does have a very decent roll of honour. Since the mid 1960s, Tom Watson has won it five times, Tiger Woods, Jack Nicklaus, Seve Ballesteros and Nick Faldo have all won it three times, while Greg Norman and Padraig Harrington have been repeat winners. There is a rota of Open courses: St Andrews, Carnoustie, Turnberry, Troon and Muirfield in Scotland and Royal Lytham, Royal Liverpool, Royal Birkdale and Royal St George's in England. All courses are set up fairly, and it's the conditions that determine the difficulty of the week. You need a player that is comfortable in the wind, is imaginative with their clubs and able to employ an array of shots. In 2004, Todd Hamilton was another 750/1 winner of the Open at Troon. At least somebody had something on him – one gentleman had £20 each way with Stan James – and Hamilton was a winner on the US Tour that year. Since then, Woods has won twice, Harrington has won twice, and I've talked about Cink and Oosthuizen. I remember Nick Price had two very near misses before winning in 1994 and although he hasn't won it yet, a player like Sergio Garcia interests me in the Open. The Spaniard's runner-up finish to Harrington in 2007 was one of six Top 10 finishes in fourteen starts up to 2010.

Looking ahead, the 2011 Open Championship will be staged at Royal St George's in Sandwich, Kent, where Ben Curtis shocked the golfing world eight years ago. Royal St George's is a tricky course, with a lot of blind shots for the players (they cannot see the flags or danger) and uneven fairways. It tests a player's mental strength. Woods and Garcia contended in 2003. In 2012, the Open will be held at Royal Lytham near Liverpool, where David Duval emerged triumphant in 2001.

Oh, one more thing. The caddie. The man who carries the bag. The caddie is often a very good golfer himself, and is tasked with reading the yardages and putts, selecting the correct clubs and ensuring the equipment is present and correct. This is what I would call real rummaging for data, but do you know who Padraig Harrington's caddie is? Or Rory McIlroy's? A player's caddie can be very underrated. Not just for expertise out on the course, but for maintaining the player's focus by keeping him relaxed in the pressure cooker. In the 1999 Open at Carnoustie, Jean Van de Velde of France came to the 18th tee in the final round with a three-shot lead. It was the 72nd and last regulation hole of the tournament and surely the Open was in the bag. France was going to have its first winner of the Open since 1907. All Van de Velde required was a double bogey, a six, to win. This was a new situation for Van de Velde. He had an inexperienced caddie. The caddie didn't hit Van de Velde over the head as he should have when his player took a driver off the tee. Van de Velde should have been more conservative, playing with a 3-wood or an iron with his first shot. The driver brought the Barry Burn into play. The tee shot went into the rough off the 17th fairway, but the ball was still dry. The next shot was critical. Instead of laying up, chipping over the stream and taking his medicine to win, Van de Velde went for the green with a two iron. His caddie did nothing. The second shot hit the grandstand and went into deep rough. Van de Velde's third shot found the stream. In images beamed around the world, he took off his shoes and socks and tried to play from the water. It was a hopeless task. The damage had been done. Van de Velde ended up making seven and losing the Open in play-off. It was a monumental breakdown. Greg Norman suffered a different type of collapse at Augusta, but this was sadder and more bewildering. Ultimately, it was Van de Velde's fault, but I wonder would history be different if he'd had a stronger caddie by his side.

## First Round Shootout

One area which I have become interested in from a golf-betting perspective is the first-round leader market. How could I not be after Lucas Glover Gate? The first round is a tournament in itself and it's a much more level playing field. Anyone can lead after the opening round, when players don't look at scoreboards, are not as nervous and just want to get themselves into position.

I took a chance each way on Peter Hanson at 100/1 for the 2010 Open and he ended in a tie for fourth position, giving a dead-heat return of about 14/1 for the place when taking ties into account. Hanson had finished 13th at the US Open and came into the Open as an improving player. He could handle windy conditions, he was a winner on the European Tour and had a consistent swing which meant he made a lot of cuts. When I'm looking for first-round leaders I always check a player's final round the week before, because a low round can give a player momentum. This was the case when Zach Johnson won the Colonial Tournament on the US PGA Tour in 2010. He'd missed the cut at the Texas Open, but it was after rounds of 80 and 68. He then shot 65 on day one at Colonial. JB Holmes did something very similar at the 2010 Quail Hollow Championship, missing the cut with rounds of 79 and 68, before shooting a 66 in the opening round of the Players Championship. I will never forget how the veteran Joey Sindelar won the Quail Hollow Championship in 2004. I was trying to work out how he had found his game, but noticed that his final round the week before was a low one. Momentum counts when examining golfers for a staking plan. It's worth adding to the list.

## The US PGA

I was working in a London bank to pay my way through university when Davis Love III won the 1997 US PGA Championship at Winged Foot. It was my first ever winner on a golf tournament. My brother-in-law made me curious, as I was staying with him that summer. He'd backed Jesper Parnevik at 66/1 in the Open the previous month, and we both watched Parnevik finish second behind Justin Leonard. I had been watching golf for years, but never put any money down. I was intrigued, so I had £5 on Davis Love III and Phil Mickelson ahead of the next major, the US PGA. Love then went and won the tournament easily at 33/1, much to my astonishment at the time. £170 was a lot of money for an eighteen-year-old. It didn't matter what the stake was – I had picked a winner! – and I could hop on the Tube and go shopping. I haven't backed the winner of the PGA since.

Martin Kaymer should have changed all that in 2010 when he won the Wannamaker Trophy by beating Bubba Watson to win at Whistling Straits, but I messed up. When you are a little off your game, it can be the difference between winning and losing a lot of money. You just have to remain calm and wait for the good breaks. Kaymer had already won five times on the European Tour before teeing it up at the PGA. What was clear when sizing up the twenty-five-year-old German was that he possessed Teutonic *cojones*. He is what I call a 'closer'. He should win many more majors. His talent was on my radar and I selected him as one of my tips for the 2010 US Open, the tournament McDowell won. One advantage of backing a golfer is that they become one of your children for four days. You agonise over every shot, every putt, with quiet nods of approval when the leaderboard on the computer gives you good news and flashes of irritation when a double bogey is carded.

Backing golfers for small money can be really beneficial down the line as you learn so much about their games. Kaymer was 8th at the US Open, just out of the money for the each way part of the bet, but it was a very promising performance at 80/1. I noticed that he putted very well, but made some unforced errors on certain holes. He'd also remarked in an interview earlier in the year that he'd probably need some time to make it in America, and cope with the demands of the majors. I observed Kaymer at the Open, when I didn't back him.

He played out of his skin to shoot level par on the back nine at St Andrews on the windy Friday, but what disconcerted me was his three bogeys on the final three holes on the Sunday. I was thinking "Not Ready".

On the final day of the US PGA, Kaymer took control, but he began to experience turbulence by missing shots and putts down the stretch. Dustin Johnson was on his way to a one-shot lead with a birdie on 17 and Kaymer needed to hole a 15-foot putt on the 18th to match Bubba Watson in the clubhouse. He buried the putt in the hole. Johnson was subsequently slapped with a two-shot penalty for grounding his club in a bunker on the 18th, so it was just Watson and Kaymer in extra holes. I knew Watson was mentally fragile and when Kaymer drained another putt in the play-off, the colour drained from my face. So, like Harrington at the 2007 Open, once Kaymer got a second bite, he didn't let go.

They call the US PGA 'Glory's Last Shot' and of all the majors, it's the least glamorous. Cruelly, some have labelled it as an easier, uglier version of the US Open, but the PGA of America have got their act together since the late 1990s. The courses utilised for the PGA are much better than they were and it's a tough but fair event. One important statistic when examining Kaymer's win was that he was a winner in 2010, at the Abu Dhabi Championship. David Toms in 2001, Rich Beem in 2002 and YE Yang were all unlikely winners of the US PGA, especially in the case of Beem and Yang, but all three had won on the US Tour in the year of their victories. Yang was a 200/1 shot at Hazeltine in 2009. Harrington had just won the Open and was 20/1 in a Tigerless field when he came out on top at Oakland Hills. So he was in form. Shaun Micheel, the 2003 winner and John Daly, in 1991, were complete shocks, but between 2004 and 2007, Tiger Woods won twice, while Vijay Singh and Phil Mickelson were also successful.

Looking ahead to the 2011 US PGA Championship at the Atlanta Athletic Club, there's not much to go on, given Toms and Mickelson had the event to themselves the last time the rota visited Georgia in 2001. What is true about Toms and Mickelson is that they are exceptional iron players and putters. In general, you need to highlight a player happy with his game who is suited to the demands of the course in question. Any positive memories of the course from past visits are a bonus. Kaymer hadn't played Whistling Straits in 2004, but he flew to Wisconsin with a great golf game and a winning mentality. It was all the baggage he needed.

# Chapter 11

## *Yankee Golf Lessons*

Outside of the Majors, I limit my golf betting to the US PGA Tour. "These Guys Are Good" is its catchphrase, and it has grown into a juggernaut over the last decade, assisted by the increased popularity of golf as a spectator sport since the Tiger Woods era began in 1996. The United States hosts three of the four recognised 'Major Championships' – three World Golf Championships (WGC events) and the prestigious Players Championship. The TV networks including NBC and CBS are behind it and, despite the recession, there are enough sponsors to ensure huge paydays for tournament winners. We are talking around one million dollars per victory. Briny Baird, a regular on the tour for over 300 starts, has banked over $11 million in his career without winning as this book goes to print. What is even more flabbergasting and, frankly, a little obscene, is that Furyk was given a cheque for 10 million dollars for winning the end-of-season FedEx Cup series in 2010. So as good as the European Tour is, for me as a bettor, the PGA Tour is 'the show'.

I don't back on the European Tour. It's important to specialise and I would rather devote my attention to the United States, where the fields are better and to my mind the results make more sense. That's not to say the European Tour is poor – the Race to Dubai has increased its appeal, but Padraig Harrington, Rory McIlroy and Graeme McDowell know the importance of playing in America, for testing themselves against the very best and getting the right preparation for three of the four majors. Harrington, Justin Rose, Paul Casey and Luke Donald stayed in America to play PGA tournaments in August and September in 2010 rather than return home for the European events which could have qualified them automatically for the Ryder Cup team. The landscape may be changing, with Lee Westwood, Martin Kaymer and Rory McIlroy all committing themselves to playing on the European Tour in 2011, but they will still compete in the big American events, and my focus is not on the merits of one tour against another. It's about making money.

So, using the tools from Chapter 6, here is a run down of all of the US PGA Tour events as currently constructed from January until September.

## January

### Hyundai Tournament of Champions, Plantation Course, Kapalua, Hawaii

This is an interesting event because it is exclusively for winners from the previous year. So the field is generally a quarter of a regular tour event, which means you should get involved, as the odds are more in your favour. Tiger Woods and Phil Mickelson usually skip it. In 2010, there were only twenty-eight entrants and the winner Geoff Ogilvy (9/1) had won the tournament in 2009, so his form at the Plantation Course was obvious. Ogilvy and Stuart Appleby (a three-time winner from 2004 to 2006) are Australians, so rust is not as much of an issue with them given their commitments to events 'down under' around Christmas time. Appleby was 28/1 to defend in 2005 and 14/1 in 2006. They were generous prices considering his course form. It's a course that suits long drivers, a par 73, with big greens. The greens consist of Bermuda grass, which they also play on in Florida. Accuracy off the tee is not important. It's also an exposed course at Kapalua, so you need to keep in mind good wind players.

## Sony Open, Waialae Country Club, Honolulu, Hawaii

2010 winner Ryan Palmer (175/1) was a real head-scratcher, as he had missed the cut on two previous visits to Honolulu and his best posting was Tied 28th. It's a par 70, and there is more rough than Kapalua. A player must hit many greens in regulation to contend. The putting surfaces are Bermuda and it can get windy. There have been some short-priced winners, like Ernie

Els (10/1 in 2004) and Vijay Singh (6/1 in 2005), but Paul Goydos was a 250/1 bomb in 2007. It's the first event of the year for many, so treat it with caution. I do follow players with course form, as Pat Perez has always given me a run for my money here, and got me some each-way dough in 2008.

### Bob Hope Classic, California

A tricky event in that it is what I would call a putting competition with some really low scoring. It's also a pro-am and played on different courses over five days, with amateurs partnering the professionals until the final day. 2010 winner Bill Haas had four previous finishes ranging from Tied 16th to Tied 34th, which was respectable for a young gun in a shootout tournament. Thus his winning price of 100/1 was generous. You need a player who makes a bunch of birdies and eagles and murders the par 5s. So look at birdie stats. This is the tournament that caused indigestion when Perez (who I didn't back) won at 66/1 in 2009 after I tipped him on air the previous week. DJ Trahan won at 200/1 in 2008 and Charley Hoffman was a 125/1 winner in 2007, so don't be scared of outsiders.

### Farmers Insurance Open (formerly Buick Invitational), Torrey Pines, California

I remember backing John Daly in 2004 early in the season, sensing a comeback was on the cards. I was in Paris on Valentine's weekend covering

France v Ireland when Daly broke my heart more than any girl could by winning at 150/1. I hadn't backed him and he won. This event is played on two courses, Torrey Pines North and Torrey Pines South. They use the easy North course and the harder South course for the first two rounds, and then only the South course for the weekend. Poa Annua greens are used, so be aware of Californians who are comfortable with the surfaces. The South course hosted the US Open in 2008, so the total driving stat is important and you need a decent scrambler on your side. 2010 winner Ben Crane finished Tied 7th in 2009, but still went off at 80/1. Tiger Woods loves this tournament and he won it four years in a row from 2005 to 2008, going off at 5/4 in 2008.

## February

### Waste Management Phoenix Open, TPC of Scottsdale, Arizona

This tournament is usually held on Super Bowl weekend. My view of Phoenix is that players who like it – the course and the general rowdiness that is on show from the fans – lap it up, while others just can't cut it. It's a desert course with many bunkers. You don't need to be too accurate off the tee, but good performance on the par 4s and hot putting is essential. The type of player who wins here is mixed. JB Holmes won in 2006 at 200/1 and then returned to win in 2008 at 100/1. What a bizarre price for somebody who had already won the event! Never in a million years would that happen in any other sport. Aaron Baddeley would come into my mind as the type of player who would do well here, as his putting is superb and he won in 2007 at 125/1. 2010 winner Hunter Mahan (66/1) wouldn't strike me as a typical winner in Phoenix, but he did have one Top 10 finish from four starts at the course.

## Pebble Beach Pro-Am, California

This is played on a rota of courses (Pebble Beach, Spyglass Hill and Monterey Peninsula) and it can be wet on the coast of California early in the year, leading to bumpy Poa Annua greens, on which some players struggle. It's a pro-am, so some players don't like that either. The greens at Pebble Beach are small, so bear in mind good scramblers. I backed the winner in 2006, Arron Oberholser, at 33/1. It was a no-brainer, as he had been 4th and 6th in his previous two visits and came into the event in form. Dustin Johnson won in 2010 for the second year in a row, at 22/1. Phil Mickelson took the title in 2005 and 2007. His 2007 odds were 14/1. Once again, another magnificent victory for advocates of course form.

## Northern Trust Open (formerly Nissan Open), Riviera, California

This is a real shotmaker's course, so good ball-striking is important. Hitting greens is the key – accuracy off the tee less so. Eight major champions have won this event in the last twenty years, so look for experienced players who know how to plot their way around. Liking the track is also beneficial, as 2010 winner Steve Stricker proved. He went off at 14/1 having finished 2nd in 2009. Stricker also finished 3rd in Hawaii before his victory. Phil Mickelson won in 2008 and 2009 and was a bigger price in 2009 (16/1). Why? I don't know.

## WGC – World Matchplay Championship, Dove Mountain, Arizona

This is matchplay, so it requires some macho. You can't be a wimp when you only have one opponent – and strokeplay form isn't crucial. 2010 winner Ian Poulter is certainly a very in-your-face type of golfer – and given his superb performance at the 2008 Ryder Cup (also in Matchplay Format), he was a decent price at 28/1. He also had reached the quarter finals in this event at Dove Mountain on two separate occasions. The course sets up well for those who like to gamble, with all of the par 5s reachable in two shots, but there are plenty of bunkers. However the main opponent in matchplay is the man, not the course. Geoff Ogilvy has won this a couple of times, in 2006 and 2009 – in 2009 he was 25/1. Look for good matchplayers, in the Ryder Cup and in the Presidents Cup.

### Mayakoba Golf Classic, El Camaleon, Mexico

Not a lot to say about this one, given it is on the same week as the Matchplay, but 2010 winner Cameron Beckman went off at 100/1 after finishes of 7th and Tied 15th from three previous visits to the course. He was out of form, but his fond memories of the venue paid dividends. It's a par 70 course, designed by Greg Norman, which is suited to accurate players.

## March

### Honda Classic, PGA National, Florida

Camilo Villegas won this in 2010 at 30/1. He was in the semi-finals of the World Matchplay and finished in the Top 10 in Phoenix, so his game was in decent shape. He also finished Tied 2nd at PGA National in 2007, so there were plenty of things in his favour. PGA National staged the 1983 Ryder Cup and 1987 US PGA, so it's a marquee course, that doesn't give up scores easily to the par of 70. The fairways are tight, which means that good driving is important. Water is present and the course is heavily bunkered. Bermuda grass is used, so players based in Florida tend to do well. YE Yang and Todd Hamilton have won major championships at huge odds in the same year after taking the Honda Classic, so keep an eye on the winner.

**WGC – CA Cadillac Championship, Doral, Florida**
It can get windy at Doral, but the course is generous. Ernie Els won this in 2010 at 35/1. He came into the tournament after a decent start to the season (with three finishes inside the top 12) before going off the boil. You have to remember that with the biggest names their natural talent can allow them to push the reset button quicker than everyone else. Els' recent record at Doral had been mediocre, but he won at the course in 2002, so that would have been a positive. I backed and tipped Ogilvy here at 40/1 in 2008. Els, Woods and Phil have all won it. I hear cream rising to the top.

**Puerto Rico Open, Trump International Golf Club**
Another tournament that is in the shadow of a World Golf Championship, played in the same week. Tour rookie Derek Lamely won this at 125/1 in 2010. Delving deeper, Lamely came off the secondary Nationwide Tour to win his card for the 'big show' as it were. Importantly, he had won on the Nationwide in 2009 and as I've said before, winning is winning. He also made two PGA Tour appearances in 2009 and one of them was in Puerto Rico, where he was Tied 13th. A

classic example of how research can pay off. Lamely was a surprise, because not many players win so soon, but Michael Bradley won here in 2009 at 250/1, so taking a plunge is okay at a par 72 layout which yields low (good) scores.

### Transitions Championship, Copperhead Course, Florida

Jim Furyk won in 2010 at 35/1. It wouldn't have been easy to select him, as his form going in was average and he could only finish Tied 52nd in 2009. He did throw in a round of 65 in that finish, so it's important when taking into account past results of a player at a course to examine their low scores. If a player cannot break 70 somewhere, he may not like how the place fits his eye. This is a paradise for robotic fairways and greens players, such as Furyk, 2009 winner Retief Goosen and 2005 winner Carl Pettersson. There are five par 3s in the total par of 71. You need to consult total driving and greens in regulation statistics.

### Arnold Palmer Invitational (formerly Bay Hill Invitational), Orlando, Florida

Arnold Palmer changed the layout from a par 70 to a par 72 for 2010, to allow the players find more birdies, but the winner Ernie Els only posted 11 under par. It's a typical Florida venue, with plenty of water and bunkers. Els went off at odds of 20/1. We know that he was in form, with a victory in the same state two weeks before he teed it up in Arnold's backyard. Els also won this event in 1998, so course form wasn't an issue. Tiger Woods has won six times at Bay Hill.

## April

**Houston Open, Redstone, Humble, Texas**
They have moved this tournament to the week before the Masters to attract better players, so the course is framed to resemble Augusta. This was one week in 2010 where I backed a golfer – Anthony Kim at 25/1 – but didn't tip him on air. Kim was Tied 5th in his first appearance in Houston in 2007 and was a much better player in 2010. He also finished second behind Villegas at the Honda, so for me he was a confident choice. In the week before a major, some players prefer to work on their games so beware if you are looking to back someone you fancy for a major. Paul Casey, Adam Scott and Stuart Appleby would be power players in my mind, and they have all won at this par 72 layout.

**US Masters, Augusta (See Chapter 10)**

**Texas Open, Oaks Course, San Antonio, Texas**
Another tournament which has been shifted in the calendar, from September/October to April. Justin Leonard has won it three times, in 2000, 2001 and

2007. In 2007 he was available at 33/1. Zach Johnson, a major winner, was 66/1 when he won in 2008. And he repeated the feat in 2009 at 14/1. Adam Scott won in 2010 in his first appearance at 25/1. The Oaks course also staged the tournament for the first time in 2010. Hitting shots in the right areas of the undulating greens is key at this course. Eric Axley and Robert Gamez were 250/1 winners in Texas in the noughties and 200/1 rags Bart Bryant and Tommy Armour III also took home the silver. Not the best tournament to place your last nickel on.

### Heritage, Harbour Town, South Carolina
I love this tournament as I have just come off watching the Masters and I'm in the mood for watching golf and following investments. It's a very tight track, with some of the smallest greens on tour, so keep an eye out for players who hit a lot of greens and can scramble well. It can also get quite windy, but low scores are frequent nowadays. Jim Furyk, a recent winner at the Transitions Championship, won this in 2010 at 16/1. He had placed 2nd at Harbour Town in 2005 and 2006. Boo Weekley won this in consecutive years, in 2007 and 2008, and was 40/1 for that repeat success in 2008.

### New Orleans Classic, Avondale, Louisiana
Ah, yes, home of the Flesch win. But English Turn, where Flesch won, was sacrificed for Avondale, where the event has been staged in recent years.

80/1 shot Jason Bohn won in a weak field in 2010. He had a finish of Tied 20th and three missed cuts in four previous starts in the 'Big Easy' and that was not exactly inspiring. He did finish Tied 11th in Houston, which would have given clues about the state of his golf. Not a tournament I like to get heavily involved in. Andrés Romero won on his first look in 2008 at 125/1 and Jerry Kelly, who wins every ten years, was the 150/1 shock in 2009. Accuracy is not important off the tee at the par 72 Avondale, but hitting greens is.

## May

### Wells Fargo Championship (formerly Wachovia), Quail Hollow, North Carolina

This is the tournament in which Rory McIlroy announced his American arrival in 2010, nearly missing the cut and then playing what I would describe as 'PlayStation' golf on the weekend, shooting 16 under par on one of the tougher layouts to win at 66/1. McIlroy was in a bit of a funk, so it was a victory for natural talent. This is one of the best tournaments of the year at a par 72 course which rewards good ball-striking, so follow the results. Lucas Glover performed well at Quail Hollow before winning the US Open and another great tee to green merchant, Sean O'Hair, was a 50/1 winner in 2009.

## The Players Championship, Sawgrass, Florida

Do you know that 'The Players' is now held in May rather than March and that they tinkered with the course in 2007? These things matter, as the organisers want more of a 'major' feel, for what they see as the 'fifth major'. This is the PGA Tour's signature event, and it carries a stronger line-up than most of the majors. The organisers, in bringing a bit more rough into play and altering the greens at the par 72 at Sawgrass, sought firm and fast conditions and more of a test off the tee. Padraig Harrington finished 2nd twice, nearly winning in 2004, but I don't think he likes the changes. Tiger Woods won in 2001, but his other displays have not been stellar. 2010 winner Tim Clark was a 100/1 chance and he liked the tailoring, which suited his accurate play. Clark was Tied 9th the year before he won. He was 2nd at the Bob Hope before his form deserted him for a while. 2009 winner Henrik Stenson was a 50/1 shot, after finishing Tied 10th the year before. And Sergio Garcia, who was 2nd in 2007 in the first year of the revamp, won in 2008 at 40/1! I backed Robert Allenby at 100 on Betfair in 2010 and he was a close 2nd. He had all the attributes I was looking for – a fourth-placed finish at the course in 2003, a brilliant long game and a background in Australia playing tough courses – but he found Clark too good. I also had him for a place. It's betting suicide, or just greedy, not to go each way on any golfer.

## Crowne Plaza Invitational at Colonial, Fort Worth, Texas

When Tim Clark and Steve Marino went into a three-way play-off for the 2009 Colonial with Steve Stricker, I was patting myself on the back, after putting up Clark at 33/1 and Marino at 60/1 each way on the radio before the tournament began. To my chagrin, Stricker won the play off. I backed Zach Johnson to win this in 2010, but it was a personal bet at 55/1. He was Tied 9th in 2009 and had three other finishes in the Top 30 at Colonial. A player like Johnson is always worth having on your side as he wins, goes away for a while, and then wins. Good putting is the key, I think. I also had a personal bet on Steve Flesch in this event at 60/1 in 2004. I love this tournament. It suits players who keep the ball straight. Driving distance is not a factor. It's an old-style course over a par of 70 with many doglegs. It hasn't changed much since golfers played with wooden clubs. Tiger Woods doesn't fancy it.

## Byron Nelson Championship, TPC Four Seasons Resort, Irving, Texas

I try to keep an eye on the Nationwide and Q School graduates as they begin life on the US PGA Tour, reading articles, analysing statistics and trawling for interview transcripts. I knew Jason Day won a Nationwide Tour event at the age of only 19, which was partly why I recommended some each-way money on him earlier in the year. And in his first Byron Nelson, he won at 150/1. In hindsight, I should have backed him blind every week until he won, but you can't do that with every rookie. At the time of writing, American Ryder Cup stars Rickie Fowler and Jeff Overton have yet to win on tour. The Byron Nelson is not my favourite event. You need a player to sink a lot of birdies, because winning scores tend to be low. It can generate shock winners, such as Ted Purdy at 200/1 in 2005, Brett Wetterich at 100/1 a year later, and Scott Verplank at 80/1 in 2007. I like to keep the stakes small for this one.

## June

### Memorial Tournament, Muirfield Village, Ohio

This tournament is in the top bracket of tour events. It's hosted by the 'Golden Bear' – Jack Nicklaus. Unfortunately for him, he captained the USA when Europe beat them in the 1987 Ryder Cup at Muirfield Village. The place reminds me a bit of Augusta. It's a course that puts a premium on the second shot, where irons from the fairway must be struck crisply and in the right place. I knew Justin Rose loved Muirfield Village before he won me €2,000 off a €25 stake in 2010. He had referred to it as his favourite course in interviews, and he had the record to back that up, with a Tied 2nd finish in 2008 and a 4th in 2004.

He was 10th at the European Tour's PGA Championship at Wentworth, so form wasn't an issue going in. And Rose has also got a good record at the Masters. Another Master, Tiger Woods, has won four times at Muirfield Village, and fellow victors Kenny Perry and Ernie Els have mirrored their Memorial wins with good performances at Augusta. Bart Bryant was a 250/1 stunner in 2005 and Carl Pettersson was a 150/1 shot when he finished top of the pile a year later, so I wouldn't put you off a reconnaissance for value. A rookie has never won the event.

## St Jude Classic, Southwind, Tennessee

One of the lesser-known stops, but it's played at the same course, so that helps for your historical research. Lee Westwood won on his first appearance in the tournament in 2010 at 13/1, and that was a victory down to class, as Westwood is the current world number one as I write this in November 2010. Southwind is a suffocating par 70 where you need to avoid the penal rough. If you can do that, it's fine. I remember backing 2006 winner Jeff Maggert before the final round at 20/1. Sometimes odds compilers get it wrong, because one brilliant round can change everything. Maggert shot 65 that day to win. Flesch was 66/1 entering the final round when he won for me in New Orleans in 2003, a bigger price than he was quoted before the tournament. David Toms won this tournament in 2003 and 2004 and was

20/1 the second time around. Justin Leonard was also a dual winner, in 2005 and 2008 and was available at 33/1 both times.

## US Open (See Chapter 10)

## Travelers Championship (formerly Greater Hartford Open), Connecticut

I've already recanted the Bubba Watson debacle. I remember Hunter Mahan played really well at the 2007 US Open, finishing 13th. When a new face does well at a major, it gives them tremendous confidence and, in Mahan's case, he won this tournament on his next start at 70/1. Stewart Cink and Phil Mickelson have both won this event twice. Driving Distance is a key statistic at the par 70 course at River Highlands and as the course is straightforward, also look for good putters.

# July

## AT & T National, Aronimink Golf Club, Pennsylvania

This was a new course, as Congressional in Maryland was closed in preparation for the 2011 US Open. It was a course where ball-striking was paramount and Justin Rose, at 30/1, played incredibly to win again. What was interesting was that he led the Travelers by a street the week before at halfway, before collapsing with a final round 75. For Rose to show the mental fortitude to come back and win a week later was very impressive, and worthy of any notebook entry.

## John Deere Classic, TPC Deere Run, Illinois

What I like about this tournament is that it's held every year at Deere Run, unlike other events which switch venues from time to time. So 2009 winner Steve Stricker was always going to be a good bet for anyone who backed him, and he obliged in 2010 at 16/1. The field isn't strong so, on the one hand, classier contenders such as Vijay Singh or Kenny Perry have obliged, but there have also been 6 first-time winners on tour in this event in the last twelve years. Low scores are commonplace, so your selection must make birdies. I backed John Senden in this event in 2006. I just had an inkling as his stats were fantastic, he was playing well, and he liked the course. He won at 66/1, ensuring a greater degree of Veuve Cliquot consumption that month.

## Open Championship (See Chapter 10)

## Canadian Open, St George's, Ontario

A difficult week for punters in 2010 in that the St George's course had not been used for this tournament since 1968. Oh, Canada. Carl Pettersson won at 80/1. His form was patchy going in, but he did finish 6th at the AT & T. And it was his fourth tour victory, so he knew what was needed on the closing nine. 14 under par ended up as the winning score, so it wasn't US Open tough. The 2011 Canadian Open will be played at the Shaughnessy Golf Club, which held the tournament back in 2005. Mark Calcavecchia won that year with a winning score of just 5 under par. Ryan Moore, who is a much better player now, was 2nd.

### Greenbrier Classic, White Sulphur Springs, West Virginia

This was a new tournament in 2010, and when that happens, you have to concentrate on those who are playing well. 2010 winner Stuart Appleby was in and out of form, but then shot the round of his life, a 59, to take victory over Jeff Overton, who was in form, and only a 25/1 chance. Appleby was returned at 75/1. It was his ninth US victory, so a consistent 'winner' is always good to have on your side. A winning score of 22 under par suggests an easy track.

## August

### WGC – Bridgestone Invitational, Firestone, Ohio

I went and tipped Tiger Woods going into this one in 2010, and that was very much the wrong move, as in a tournament which he had won seven times and never finished worse than fifth, he ended up on 18 over par after four rounds. I couldn't have made a worse call. Woods' total was 30 shots behind 2010 winner Hunter Mahan, who had showed a steady state of improvement at Firestone, finishing Tied 22nd, Tied 10th and Tied 4th in successive years before taking the title. That type of trend is worth noting. Of course Mahan won in Phoenix, so he's comfortable with Sunday heat and warmed up for this tournament with a Tied 17th finish in Canada. The lesson with Woods is that a golfer needs to be focused on the job in hand, whatever their talent. As for Firestone – it tests all aspects of a game. It's long and hitting greens is paramount.

## Reno Tahoe Open, Montreux Golf Club, Nevada

This was held on the same week as the Open in 2010, and it produced 200/1 winner Matt Bettencourt. He had no discernible form to rely upon going into the event and was 53rd on his only previous appearance. His winning score was 11 under par, so the Montreux course, which is a par 72, is not a pushover. Vaughn Taylor was a 50/1 repeat winner in 2005 following his 2004 victory. That was a price which really beggared belief. Will McKenzie was a 300/1 winner of this event in 2006. There is a random element to these lesser tournaments which I don't like, as it's harder to reach the end of the rainbow.

## US PGA Championship (See Chapter 10)

## Wyndham Championship, Sedgefield, North Carolina

200/1 longshot Arjun Atwal won in 2010 after missing the cut the year before, although he did shoot 67 on the second day in 2009 before departing. This has been held at Sedgefield since 2008, and before Atwal, solid ballstrikers Carl Pettersson and Ryan Moore were victorious. Winning scores are low at this course, so it's another putting competition, with tee shots more important than hitting greens. Length is not a factor. Moore was a decent price at 66/1 for his maiden tour win. I didn't back him, but I was following his career closely. He was the best amateur in the USA, but suffered from a hand injury which stymied his progress for a while.

## The Barclays, Plainfield Country Club, New Jersey

This is the first of the four play-off events for the Fed Ex Cup, so all the top names are involved for the $10 million bounty. Matt Kuchar won this in 2010 at 35/1 when it was held at Ridgewood Country Club. You could have backed Kuchar, following his good early play at the US PGA, excellent all round statistics, and record of ten Top 10 finishes entering the event. I tipped Kevin Streelman at 175/1 on Twitter each way on the basis that the only time the event was played in Ridgewood in 2008, he finished Tied 4th. He had local knowledge of the course and played solidly at the Wyndham, so his Tied 3rd finish behind Kuchar generated an each-way pay-out at 44/1. Kuchar missed the cut in 2008, which illustrates the importance of recent form.

This tournament will be held at a new course, Plainfield, in New Jersey in 2011, so look for in-form players.

## September

### Deutsche Bank Championship, TPC of Boston, Massachusetts

This tournament has been played at the TPC of Boston since emerging in 2003 with a tendency to give up low scores. There is a mixture of the familiar and the bizarre when it comes to the roll of honour. Vijay Singh has won twice, while Tiger Woods and Phil Mickelson have also succeeded, but Olin Browne took the title in 2005 at 200/1 and our latest winner in 2010, Charley Hoffman, was a 140/1 shot. Hoffman's best finish in Boston was Tied 27th, so you would have to have been pretty prescient to pick him. His game was in good enough shape, with a Tied 7th at the John Deere and a Tied 4th in Canada. It can get windy, but apart from that, the course is there for the taking.

## BMW Championship (formerly Western Open), Cog Hill, Illinois

Dustin Johnson gained a deserved victory in 2010, at odds of 33/1, which were generous considering he nearly won both the US Open and US PGA. Johnson finished Tied 30th at Cog Hill in 2009, but it's not about stats, it's about interpretation of the stats. When Johnson is on, he is on. He hits it miles and he putts well and at Cog Hill, good driving and putting come to the fore. Cog Hill is a classic course and the rough is severe. Tiger Woods has won this tournament five times and good competitors such as Camilo Villegas and Trevor Immelman have also claimed victory just outside Chicago.

## Tour Championship, East Lake, Atlanta, Georgia

This is the final event of the Fed Ex series and the last big gathering for the top names until the HSBC Champions in Shanghai in November. The field is whittled down to 30 by this stage, so there's magnificent value to be had as a punter. Jim Furyk won his third PGA Tour event of the year in 2010 at odds of 22/1. It was his first Tour Championship success (he was second at East Lake behind Adam Scott in 2006). They have made the course tougher in recent years; in the last three renewals the winning score was less than 10 under par. So your guy needs to hit the fairway and putt well on the slick greens in

Atlanta. For a tournament that only has 30 players, it can produce some big prices. Phil Mickelson won in 2009 at 25/1, which was amazing considering who he is and his fondness for the course (he won in 2000). And I know Bart Bryant was an outsider in 2005, but if he was good enough to make the final 30 by winning the Memorial Tournament, he was good enough to win – and he did, at 100/1.

## The European Tour

I won't be disingenuous enough to peddle myself as some type of European Tour expert, because I am not, but *quelle surprise*, course and recent form does play a part in explaining a good chunk of the winners.

The PGA Championship, or the BMW Championship, as it is known, is the flagship event on the European Tour – held in Wentworth, just outside London in May. Wentworth is a tough, tree-lined course, and you need to have a good long game to function at it. Simon Khan won in 2010 on a sponsor's exemption at 200/1, which surprised me when I was doing some post-tournament research. Khan had finished 2nd in the event in 2006 and Tied 10th in 2008. He didn't have a Top 20 on his résumé all year going to Wentworth, but found his game on a course which he liked. And course form has mattered at Wentworth. Angel Cabrera won in 2005 after finishing 2nd in 2001 and 2004. Anders Hansen, the 2002 winner, won again in 2007 at 100/1. On the other hand, Scott Drummond, a 500/1 shot, ranked 435th in the world, took the title on his tournament debut in 2004. That's what I sometimes find baffling about the European Tour. Jeppe Huldahl, ranked 377th in the world, won the 2010 Wales Open at 400/1 at the Ryder Cup course, a year after Scott Strange took the same event at 150/1. Such anomalies draw me to the other side of the Atlantic.

What I can say about the European Tour is that the players at the top tend to win repeatedly. Before he became a major champion, Martin Kaymer had made his mark on the European Tour and in 2010 (in addition to the US PGA Championship) he won in Abu Dhabi, took the Dutch Open and plundered the Dunhill Links Championship. Charl Schwartzel won in consecutive weeks in January, landing the Africa Open and the Joburg Open at odds of 9/1 on each outing. Robert Karlsson won the Qatar Masters at 66/1. That was a surprise after he had sustained an eye injury, but the Swede did have a 2nd place finish to his name at the course. Miguel Angel Jimenez performed poorly in Qatar, but then won the Dubai Desert Classic at 66/1. Jimenez is a prolific operator in Europe, with 18 tour wins to his name – and he had form at the course, with two runner-up finishes. Jimenez would go on to win twice more in the remainder of 2010.

From a recent form standpoint, Rhys Davies took the Trophée Hassan in March at 33/1 having finished 3rd in Malaysia two weeks previously. Louis Oosthuizen was second to Davies in that event, and won the following week in Andalucia at 20/1. Thomas Bjorn finished Tied 9th in Wales before winning the Portugal Open the following week at 40/1. José Manuel Lara was 4th at the Dutch Open in September and then won the Austrian Open at 66/1 seven days later.

And what about our own tournament, the Irish Open? Ross Fisher won this in 2010 at 20/1, which I felt was a short price, as this was the first visit of the tournament to Killarney since 1992. With no recent course form to go on, every punter was taking it a little on trust. Fisher was in decent order, with a 2nd at the BMW International Open and an 8th at the Scottish Open behind him, but the movement of the Irish Open around the country makes it a difficult betting assignment. There's no reason why you should place money on the Irish Open ahead of any other event just because it's the Irish Open.

Perhaps, for 2011, I should place cross doubles on the two golf tours. What is a cross double? If you pick out two golfers from an event in each tour, American and European, in the same week, you have selected four golfers. Aside from individual bets, you may have the following each-way combinations. For example:

A. Tiger Woods 6/1 and Darren Clarke at 33/1

B. Tiger Woods 6/1 and Shane Lowry at 50/1

C. Jim Furyk 20/1 and Darren Clarke 33/1

D. Jim Furyk 20/1 and Shane Lowry 50/1

For a €1 each way outlay, you are investing €8 (€1 Woods and Clarke win double, €1 Woods and Clarke each-way double, etc). It's also advisable to cover yourself with each-way single bets, so in the event that if Furyk wins, but both Europeans are unplaced, you would receive some return. So adding each-way singles to the mix means you have a spend in this example of €16.

Now let's say that Furyk and Lowry are both placed at 1/4 (one quarter) of the odds. That would give you a return of the following: (Furyk 6 X Lowry 13.5 + Furyk 6 + Lowry 13.5 = €100.50). If Furyk and Lowry both won, you'd be buying a fruit machine, because the return would total: (Furyk 21 X Lowry 51 + Furyk 6 X Lowry 13.5 + Furyk 21 + Furyk 6 + Lowry 51 + Lowry 13.5 = €1,243.50).

# Chapter 12

## *Soccer*

Have you studied the weather patterns in Stoke recently? Have I lost my mind, you may ask? Maybe I have, but that's a conversation for another day. In January of 2010, Fulham travelled to play Stoke City in a Premier League game. Although they were in form, Fulham had not won a league game away from home since the previous August. So what did my mind filter? January. Away. Fulham. Stoke's Christmas wasn't full of cheer; they lost away to Manchester City on St Stephen's Day and then at home to Birmingham City two days later. But aside from Birmingham, only Chelsea and Manchester United had beaten the Potters at the Britannia Stadium since the start of the season. When I open up the Premier League's fixture list for the coming week, I try and identify one game on which to bet. Usually I lay, but occasionally I cannot resist a decent back. For days I had my eye on this one. 48 hours before kick-off I took a look at the weather forecast for Stoke-on-Trent. It wasn't good. You may remember that a lot of the UK was covered in snow at the time. Ireland was experiencing similar problems, but we had no domestic soccer to watch in front of the fire and bet on. I checked the weather forecast again on the eve of the match. A severe weather warning was issued for the UK. Fulham had a 320-mile round trip. If the match went ahead – which it would at a new stadium like the Britannia – it would be freezing. The words filled my headspace once again. January. Away. Fulham. The bet was placed on Stoke at 6/4. They were 3-0 up inside 37 minutes and held on for a 3-2 win. Now that is how research and sound judgement can make you money. Unorthodox research, but research none the less. Stoke should have been Evens given the circumstances. Instead the bookmaker offered value and I snapped off his hand. And I would rather dig deep and be right on one Premier League fixture than spread my opinions too wide on five matches.

I'm not finished with Stoke. They were drawn at home against Arsenal in the Fourth Round of the FA Cup at the end of January. Arsenal manager Arsene Wenger was not best pleased with Stoke's tactics the previous season when Rory Delap's throws caused havoc and the Gunners lost 2-1 at the Britannia Stadium. So there would be sufficient needle in my mind ahead of this match. Stoke would be hungry. Would Arsenal? Normally you wouldn't back against Arsenal in a head to head against Stoke, but this was a Cup competition. Arsenal had to play Manchester United, Chelsea and Liverpool in successive weeks after the game and were still in the Champions League. Did they need an FA Cup run in the middle of all that? The teams were announced. Wenger had chosen an understrength side full of kids. Francis Coquelin, Jay Emmanuel-Thomas and Craig Eastmond were in his team. Not exactly household names. Stoke manager Tony Pulis selected his best eleven. The speed dial was immediately activated to Paddy Power. I barely kept my composure as they confirmed a price of 100/30 down the other end. The bet was stammered from my end. I was astounded by the price. "Stoke to win, please." What a bargain. Stoke won 3-1.

I have used those two examples to illustrate my philosophy behind soccer betting. I believe in simplicity. And I strongly adhere to studying the basics. Home and away form. The past record of the two teams against each other. Recent form. Injuries. Who the 22 players on the pitch will be when the game starts. Managerial objectives.

Paddy Power estimate that 50% of their online activity is now on soccer betting, and most of that is on straightforward match betting. Soccer is also the second biggest sport on Betfair. Soccer has always been a universal language and it's now muscling its way into the punter's psyche. Soccer was my first sporting love, but Tottenham Hotspur's struggles in the 1990s really wore me down. I loved Tottenham and when I fell out of love with them for a time, my love transferred to the international arena. And from a punting perspective, I've always loved the game rather than the idea of betting on it. I've worked on soccer programming in radio for years, but I've always made my betting bed with horses and golfers. So as a relatively recent convert to soccer betting, I find I am very dispassionate. And that perversely has helped my approach to the beautiful game, because although my knowledge is above average, I don't approach it with the complete arrogance which I would size up a US golf tournament or the Cheltenham Gold Cup, when nobody knows more in the room than me.

You may be a soccer expert and you may have your own method of making it pay. If it works for you, keep doing it. All I know is that I have made a personal profit of nearly €5,000 on Betfair from soccer betting in eight years. And not a word of that is false. My analysis of my Betfair account and how straightforward it was to make money has caused a seismic shift in my thinking. The soccer percentage of my overall betting-pie is going to significantly increase in the coming years. And I recommend the same for any soccer fan with decent knowledge, because, and I am loath to write this – it is easier than the nags.

Traditionally, lulled by the sneaky bookies; I would have picked up a glossy coupon in a betting shop, scribbled down ten teams at poor odds in an accumulator and hope they all would come up. Usually I would get seven or eight right and lose my bet. I realised pretty quickly that this really was 'mug' punting. You hear the odd newspaper story on a slow news day of a guy striking gold and taking the bookie to the cleaners by getting 20-odd soccer results right in a coupon, but these prepared betting slips are in your face in the shops for a reason. You have less of a chance of winning on multiples than on singles.

Most of the other options that the bookmakers place in front of you in soccer markets are distractions. I logged on to an online bookmaker to check a routine English Championship match between Leeds United and Cardiff City in October 2010. The bookmaker had 94 markets on the game. Most of them took the form of a matador's cape. Markets like correct score, number of goals, the team to have the first corner in the game, a card index for yellow and red cards, half time/full time result (which means in a Leeds v Cardiff game, you could back Leeds to lead at half time and full time), the time of the first goal up to a certain minute, penalty misses, both teams to score in the first half, which team would receive the last booking etc. It can be difficult enough to call a match result correctly without all of these other 'offers' on the table. I see bookmakers regularly creating a potential outcome of a soccer match in their shop windows to entice people in, i.e. Liverpool v Blackpool – Liverpool to win 3-0 and Steven Gerrard to score the first goal at 33/1, €10 will win you €340. Of course it will. However it is highly unlikely that the actions of 22 players and a manager who can pick a team and substitutes will make that 33/1 bet a reality. Spain won the 2010 World Cup, which was not unexpected, but could you have easily predicted on the day of the final that Andres Iniesta would have given them a 1-0 extra time win over Holland? And who in the world could have sensed that Thomas Müller would win the Golden Boot in South Africa? Or Diego Forlan the Golden Ball for best player? Keep it simple.

In my view, there are two predominant ways to make soccer betting pay: a) backing teams to win in individual matches over the 90 minutes, or b) laying teams to lose in 90 minutes to bring the draw into play as insurance. Occasionally the first goalscorer market is worth a peek as you may have a hunch about an in-form striker, or a striker that is going to start scoring again after a quiet period. I will never forget tipping Wayne Rooney to score the first goal for Manchester United against Liverpool in a Premier League game in October 2006. Rooney was in a barren spell, but I felt the tide was about to turn. I wanted to nail it *when* it happened, not when the horse had bolted. Rooney had gone nine games without a goal. I tipped him to score the first goal against the Reds. I was actually at Old Trafford for the game, but he didn't score. Then the following Saturday, when I didn't have money on, he went and scored a hat-trick at Bolton. It must have been huge odds. I wanted to smash my head off a wall repeatedly, but I didn't because I knew it would hurt.

Like any sport, utilise knowledge of the game and common sense in the hunt for profit. If you like betting on soccer, you must keep a watching brief. From years of experience, I can get away with analysis of a racecard or a golf tournament to get a sense of what is required. I don't need to see everything from the previous week, although it's better if I do. With soccer, I find that voyeurism of Sky Sports is constantly necessary. Don't rely upon second-hand information from newspaper reports. The best way you can get a sense of what will happen is by simply observing, learning and drawing your own conclusions from week to week. The phrase 'knowledge is power' may be hackneyed, but it's true. The newspapers and websites are a valuable 'assist' for injury news, statistical analysis of team selections, goals, and cards – yellow and red.

If you were to take the Premier League outright-win market in August, on the basis of the last fifteen years you would be considering only three teams: Chelsea, Manchester United and Arsenal. It's also likely that at least one of the three promoted teams is going to be relegated by the end of the season. And when the prices for those teams are so short, nine months from the settle date, in my mind it is sensible to maintain a betting focus on the short term. So when I recommend soccer bets from time to time, I do it when I see value in a two-horse race. Let me give you three successful Premier League examples from the wireless. In December 2009 I tipped Manchester City to beat Chelsea at home at odds of 7/2. It was a bet on City to beat the league leaders at the time, but I took a chance on it. City had already beaten Arsenal on their own patch, while Chelsea had lost on the road to both Wigan Athletic and Aston Villa, so a below-par display from Carlo Ancelotti's team was always possible. It was a bet on a home team solely on price. Once again I was bringing value into the equation. I thought City, who were difficult to beat under manager Mark Hughes at the time, would be shorter in the betting. City won 2-1. The next soccer bet I put forward was in January 2010, when I recommended Everton to beat Manchester City at home at just under 2/1. Roberto Mancini was not long in his new job at City following the sacking of Hughes. I felt Everton were going to go on a run and Mancini was going to suffer defeats as he looked to impart his own ideas on the squad. No David Moyes team at home deserves to be 2/1, so on price, I had to recommend it. Everton outclassed City and won 2-0. Then I sided with Chelsea in April, when they beat Manchester United at Old Trafford in what was effectively a title decider. As a rule, United don't lose at home, but Liverpool thumped them the season before and Alex Ferguson's team were going into this match just days after a crucial Champions League game away to Bayern Munich. Wayne Rooney injured himself in that match, so he missed the Chelsea game. Didier Drogba was far from injured and he buried United with Chelsea's second goal in a 2-1 win. Chelsea's price of 12/5 was too good not to take.

So there we have it. Oppose Chelsea. Back Manchester City. Oppose Manchester City. Back Chelsea. Soccer is all about selectivity, examining what you feel is value and striking at the right time depending on the circumstances. It's my belief that it's very hard to take a long-term view on soccer markets, because a team's fortunes can change so quickly.

The ability to lay soccer teams has created a huge advantage for punters in my opinion, because you now have the draw on your side. Bookmakers have introduced

'Draw No Bet' – where you get your money refunded if there is a draw – and the odds are shorter for each team as a consequence. I prefer to lay. From time to time, you will probably get hit by laying a team which wins, but if you err on the side of caution, I believe profit is not too hard to make. It's all about reading the trends.

The best way I can explain how I lay soccer teams is to take you through what I did from March to May of 2010. I was betting frequently with small stakes of money on all sports to generate consistent data about my ideas and behaviours. I have gone through phases of not betting for months, but I wanted to know what a guinea pig felt like. The first of my sustained soccer bets was to lay Liverpool in late March away to Manchester United at just under 5/1. I have already referred to Liverpool's (4-1) win over the auld enemy the previous season, but Ferguson, who doesn't like Liverpool, was determined that wouldn't happen again and made that clear in his pre-match briefing. Watching interviews will always give you a sense of tone. Of course I could have backed United, but it was safer to take money on a Liverpool side which had not won on their travels in the league since the New Year and had lost at Wigan earlier that month. United were comfortable 2-1 winners. On the same day, I took a view with 10 minutes to go that Chelsea, having conceded an equaliser to Blackburn after 70 minutes at Ewood Park, would not win the game. Laying in-running can be a little nervy, especially if the side you lay begins to bombard the opposing goal, but I offered 2/1 and Chelsea didn't score. The next stop was League One; and with Leeds losing 1-0 to a red-hot Millwall side at Elland Road, I layed Leeds at 22/1 for small money. This lay was carried out with about twenty minutes to go. Is 22/1 risky? Not when you are watching the match and feel confident. In a horse race I may be more circumspect – in fact I remember laying a 25/1 winner many years ago – I can still remember its name, Celtic Mill – but Leeds? No. Millwall scored again to make it 2-0.

West Ham United, under boss Gianfranco Zola, were in trouble. He wasn't getting on with the owners and they had lost four games on the trot. Wolves were coming to Upton Park on the back of a win at Burnley and a draw at Aston Villa. So I layed West Ham at odds-on and heard the 'kerching' sound. I wasn't cocky enough to back Wolves and potentially lose. I would rather have layed West Ham and lost a smaller amount. At odds-on, if you lay at 6/10 (1.6) for €50, you are only liable for €30. Wolves won 3-1, incidentally. Wolves were in the middle of their 'run' which would enable them to remain in the Premier League. Winning, or not losing, breeds confidence in footballers, and teams, like the strikers which get them goals, can strike purple patches of decent form. Birmingham City went unbeaten for 12 games in the 2009-10 Premier League season between October and January, but they are not Barcelona, so it was inevitable that such a run would come to an end. After their good spell they lost away at Fulham, West Ham and Sunderland, which made me press the lay button at 3/1 when they went to Blackburn Rovers. They lost.

My first hit to a backer came about due to over-confidence. When you are at a 100% win rate, which I was, you can get involved in matters you should leave best alone. It doesn't make sense to closely analyse weather patterns in Stoke and then lay them a few months later in a careless manner. Despite the Wolves defeat, I felt West Ham were too good to go down, so I layed Stoke at odds of 3/1 in East London. Ricardo Fuller burnt my fingers with the only goal in a 1-0 Stoke win. That example of impulsiveness on a clean run wiped out a lot of my previous winnings. If you are laying regularly, you just have to take a hit on a good call on the chin, because it will happen. The key is to minimise the hits by avoiding a silly lay, as a bad call may rattle your thought processes. I tried to put the Stoke result out of my mind, and one week after losing to United, Liverpool were back at home to Sunderland. It was a match that Liverpool, despite their aimlessness at the time, were never going to lose. When Fernando Torres had the ball in the net after 3 minutes, my money was safe. It was a safe lay of Sunderland at 12/1.

You can also be lucky. I layed Barcelona against Arsenal in the Champions League at the Emirates Stadium at the end of March at 6/4. Barca should have been 10-0 up at half time. Instead, Arsenal salvaged an unlikely 2-2 draw. Another lesson of when to bet and when not to bet. You don't have to. What I was convinced about from watching the match was that Barca would make mincemeat of Arsenal in the return leg, so laying Arsenal at a much bigger price of 17/2 at the Nou Camp was a bet on much more solid ground. Note the difference in price to reflect the difference in chance. The Champions League is all about experience and I knew that Lyon, whatever the activity in the French league, had more European savvy than their quarter-final opponents Bordeaux. I confidently layed Bordeaux with success at 3/1.

Back in England (a lot of internet air-miles here) I had a bee in my bonnet about Newcastle at the time, laying them twice, at 4/5 at home to Nottingham Forest and then again at 3/4 against Blackpool. I felt that Newcastle had the Championship wrapped up, and with Forest and Blackpool chasing the play-offs, it was worth banking on Newcastle easing off. It wasn't, as the Magpies won both games. That was a case where sticking to my guns wasn't working. But when you are right, when you see a team not performing, you can make hay. I layed Sunderland at 3/1 against West Ham, taking the view that the Hammers would survive against a poor Sunderland team on the road. West Ham were turning a corner after the Stoke defeat, drawing at Everton, and they beat Sunderland 1-0. I also kept up my opposition to Birmingham City, at 19/2 away to Manchester City and layed Blackburn Rovers at 7/1 at home to Manchester United. I would have to win another 7 times at level stakes to make up for a Blackburn victory, so I had to be on the ball. A poor game at Ewood Park ended in a 0-0 draw.

When there is money down, I will watch the full 90 minutes, but apart from the entertainment, my objective is to pick up a sense of what may happen the following week. By laying successfully I was mopping up the greed of other punters on a regular basis, bringing them into a spider's web on the basis that they would take better prices than on offer with the traditional bookmakers. I could weave the web at my discretion, as long as I was making the right calls. And when I am laying and making a profit on soccer, it discourages me to back. It actually makes me more wary because I feel like I am taking more of a chance when I back something, even if the price is more attractive on the back side. I can choose to lay a team or decide that it's too risky, but the *idea* of a lay involves the least amount of risk. I escaped from the Barcelona lay at Arsenal, but such instances remind you to be selective. If you are not circumspect in soccer markets, or any markets when it comes to laying, you will get hit.

In early April, I layed Benfica in the Europa League away to Liverpool and Benfica lost 4-1. I also got involved in League One, laying Bristol Rovers at 100/30 at home to Southampton, who were on a major push for the play-offs at the time. The Saints won 5-1. That bet would have been a little out of my comfort zone and I ventured outside it again by laying Aberdeen at home to Falkirk at 11/10 and Scunthorpe against Bristol City at 6/4. Wins for Aberdeen and Scunthorpe dented my balance, so I scurried back to the Premier League. Over confidence had kicked in again due to the easy wins. I had watched Tottenham lose the F.A. Cup semi-final to Portsmouth, but my view was that my team could beat anyone on their day, so, expecting a Spurs backlash, I layed Arsenal when they came to White Hart Lane at 9/4. Spurs were due a win against Arsenal at home and they won 2-1. Then United went to City for the Manchester derby at Eastlands. United were going for the title and City were chasing fourth in the table. From what I had seen, City were far from the finished article under Mancini, so I layed them at 6/1 and they lost 1-0. I then layed City a week later at Arsenal at 3/1 and they drew. In May, I layed City at home to Tottenham and they lost 1-0. I took a very strong position on City against the big clubs and followed it through. Of course, it might not have worked out, but it was very profitable. Almost as profitable as laying every club Chelsea played at home in the Premier League under José Mourinho. He never lost a game in the league at Stamford Bridge in just over three seasons, so that would have resulted in 60 winning lays for anyone with psychic powers. Mourinho's club in the 2009-10 season was Inter Milan and as I turned my attention to the Champions League semi-finals, I had the feeling that Inter might ruffle Barcelona's feathers in the first leg at the San Siro. So I layed Barca at 6/4. Inter won 3-1. In the other semi-final, I layed Lyon away to Bayern Munich in the first leg at 11/2 and Bayern won 1-0. That was an anxious night as Bayern had Franck Ribery sent off early, but then Lyon were also reduced to 10 men before Arjen Robben scored. I felt that game proved my point about detailed bookmaker markets on matches. I left the final between Inter Milan and Bayern Munich alone. I didn't have a strong opinion on it and discipline kicked in.

So that was my behaviour on soccer markets between March and May, which netted me a soccer profit of around €2,000. I would not have become so heavily involved between August and October, because it takes time for seasonal trends to be established. Also, remember I was being a guinea pig. You may be thinking I have just given you a laundry list of bets, but I would call it a behavioural study. If I had failed miserably I would be telling you why I failed. My objective was to remain consistent in my betting and keep the search for profit simple, getting from A to B as soon as possible.

I have been concentrating on soccer in the UK, but if you have soccer knowledge on other domestic leagues, use it. I received a nice tonic after what I would describe as a quiet (nicer word for 'losing') spell on the *Ian Dempsey Show* in September 2010 when I tipped the demise of two Spanish clubs on the air. Atletico Madrid were Europa League champions but were to face Barcelona in La Liga at the weekend, so I took a chance on their opponents, Aris Salonika in Greece at 7/2. I also tipped Dinamo Zagreb at home to Villareal in Croatia at 3/1. Both of the Spanish sides lost. Unless you are dealing with Barcelona or Real Madrid, I find the lesser Spanish clubs don't possess the squad strength to field weakened teams away from home and get away with it. It's back to the weather-in-Stoke argument. You will get clubs that don't want to know, or, to be kind, are not able to cope, particularly if they have priorities elsewhere. So it doesn't matter if it's Dinamo Zagreb or

Manchester United, a winner is a winner and a tenner doesn't become a fifteen-euro note just because you have backed the outright winner of the Champions League. I enjoy being sober when it comes to soccer betting. A tenner only becomes a fifteen-euro note if I back the winner of a very select number of events which carry personal resonance such as the Cheltenham Gold Cup or the Grand National. They are my only personal exceptions!

## International Soccer

International Football is a bit enigmatic. It's more mercurial than a regular league. The performance of Greece is the seminal example. They won Euro 2004 at a price of 80/1. My 2010 World Cup tip, Brazil, capitulated like a weak South American democracy to Holland in the quarter finals, but I have had success in major tournament betting. I tipped Italy to win the 2006 World Cup at 10/1 and then Spain to win Euro 2008 at 11/2. Why?

Let's look at Italy to start.

Italy arrived in Dublin for a friendly match in August 2005 and outclassed the Republic of Ireland. The final score was 2-1 to the visitors, but Italy completely dominated the first half hour. Andrea Pirlo bossed the midfield and scored the first goal. Italy showed intent that day, more intent than you would normally see in a friendly. Before the 2006 Finals in Germany, there was a bit of a vacuum in world football. Greece were the

European Champions. France were possibly on the wane. Spain were still in an embryonic phase. Germany didn't seem to have the talent of yesteryear. England were England. Brazil and Argentina were going to try their luck on a Continent which had not produced a South American winner since 1958. So I felt Italy might be the team to fill that vacuum. Their coach Marcello Lippi had fostered a togetherness among the squad, who were all based entirely in the domestic league. As Italians, I guessed the players would be desperate to restore some pride in the jersey after the bribery scandals which had rocked Serie A that year. Italy had an immense goalkeeper in Gianluigi Buffon, a magnificent defence marshalled by Fabio Cannavaro, a ballwinner in Gennaro Gattuso in midfield, a playmaker in Pirlo, a star in Francesco Totti and an in-form physical striker in Luca Toni. I also have a personal affinity towards Italy. As a kid I skipped my dinner to dine on the exploits of Paolo Rossi. Seeing re-runs of the 1982 tournament meant I was an Italy supporter before the 1986 World Cup. So my cash went on Italy to win their fourth World Cup twenty years later.

In 2006, excluding my outright bet on Italy, I made a profit of €1,400 in personal bets on the World Cup on Betfair. I was aided by a decent chunk of capital in my account, a clear head and some annual leave. When I have the time, I approach international tournaments in quite a bold fashion, taking on what I perceive to be the weaker teams and making it my business to lay with conviction and then back odds-on shots where necessary. So I started the 2006 World Cup by laying Paraguay against England at 13/2. England were in good shape at the time and I couldn't see them losing. They prevailed by 1 goal to 0. I then watched Sweden v Trinidad and Tobago. Sweden were struggling to break down their unfancied opponents, so I layed the Scandinavians at 6/4 in the final quarter. A 0-0 draw was the end result. I then took on the Ivory Coast against Argentina at 11/2 and Serbia versus Holland at 4/1. Argentina and Holland won, boosting my account further. The beauty of a World Cup or any soccer market is that the liquidity in the Betfair market is always strong so you can back or lay for pretty much whatever you want. And when you build a bank of capital through wins, it allows you room to take the bull by the horns and cope with an occasional hit. The key is to pick your moments to get involved. So I selected the Group Stage as the place to go for it in that World Cup. 48 of the 64 matches were in the Group Stage!

Laying Angola against Portugal to me was a no-brainer, even at 14/1. The risk was obvious – a freak result and I would owe some beachbum from Brisbane or ladette from Leeds a lot of money. However, despite the colonial undertones, Angola were never going to win. I felt it was free money. Portugal won 1-0. Iran's 2006 crop was below average, so I moved to the other side of the exchange, backing Mexico at 2/3 in their match to win. I then opposed Japan against Guus Hiddink's Australia. I fancied the Socceroos, but I played safe with the lay. Australia won 3-1. I then got hit for the first time. I had taken the view that the Czech Republic were a team in decline and I layed them at even money against the USA. The Czechs won 3-0, but would come unstuck in their next two matches. So I wasn't unhappy about losing. I didn't feel I had made a dumb move. I didn't fancy Brazil with an overweight Ronaldo in their side to successfully defend their title, but they usually traverse their Group without difficulty, so I was bullish about taking on Croatia at 12/1. Once again – when laying – you have to forget about the odds or your liability and trust your judgement. I then, with success, layed both the Ukraine against Spain and Saudi Arabia in their match with Tunisia. I had no qualms about exposing myself on Togo against France at 22/1 and I made my money back on the Czechs by laying them against Italy and Ghana. And this continued well before the knockout stage.

Not every odds-on bet is a certainty. Argentina were really skinny at 2/5 to beat a half decent Mexico side in 90 minutes in the second round and I wanted to lay them. It was 1-1 after ten minutes and the Albiceleste were frustrated by the Mexicans. It took a stunner from Maxi Rodriguez to win it in extra time, but by that stage I had banked €100, exposing myself for only €40. That's how it pays to be a personal bookie at odds-on – you can take on the big hitters for a small risk and a big reward if you strike at the right time. Even when you are wrong, the prices can make for a soft landing. I wasn't keen on Germany entering the World Cup in the

Fatherland – I believed they were lucky to reach the 2002 Final and they did nothing at Euro 2004. However, as history has shown, the host nation can be inspired and Germany's manager Jurgen Klinsmann acted as a great motivator in that tournament. I layed the Germans against Poland in the Group Stage at 1/2 and was dismayed to see Oliver Neuville score in the last minute. But I didn't waver from my strategy.

After laying incessantly, I had put myself into a very strong position. It would be a profitable month regardless. That mental comfort worked against me, as I piled on Spain in the second round against France (they lost 3-1) on Argentina against Germany (they lost on penalties), and England against Portugal (they lost on penalties) in the quarter finals. I had started backing and begun to lose, which was a sign for me to get out of the tournament before I did anything silly in the remaining matches. Italy came through in the end in the outright market, but in ways that was a bonus. I had made my money early doors. And it allowed me to wear an Italian shirt that was two sizes too small and embarrass myself in a Dublin city-centre tavern during the final, singing in my best Cornetto voice once Fabio Grosso despatched the winning spot kick for the Azzurri. Repeat. Emotion after the fact. Repeat. Rinse. Repeat.

Spain were the coming team in 2008, as coach Luis Aragones had moulded some very decent young players into a winning force. It was really a solid form pick at 11/2. It would have to be, as Spain, despite some magnificent club teams, had not won a major soccer tournament in forty-four years. After a slow start, España won 8 of their last 9 matches in qualifying. Fernando Torres, David Villa, Xavi and Andres Iniesta were turning on the style and with the experienced Carlos Puyol and goalkeeper Iker Casillas at the back, it was worth taking a chance on them shedding their bridesmaid's tag. I'm always looking for the outcome which is going to happen, rather than that which has just happened.

The bookmakers are clever at making it very clear to the English public that there is a flood of patriotic money on the 'Three Lions' before a major international tourney – and as we know, they over-promise and under-deliver. England have not reached a semi-final of anything since 1990, but they perennially start in the first five in the betting for the World Cup or the European Championship. I love blind conviction from others sometimes, because it offers room to make money. I know about blind conviction; I have demonstrated it myself in the distant past. See Mickelson, Phil. The Republic of Ireland played Bulgaria in a World Cup qualifier in March 2009. We all know our national team and what Mr Trapattoni has brought to it: spirit, organisation, commitment. And when Richard Dunne opened the scoring against Bulgaria, Ireland were heavily odds-on. The beauty of in-running betting is that your eyes can help your wallet. Bulgaria began to dominate possession at Croke Park, which meant that I felt Ireland could concede. 1.32 was the number on the screen, making Ireland a 1/3 shot. I layed them and

Bulgaria then scored. So an early goal, gelled with patriotism among the Betfair backers allowed an opening for me to take a view with little exposure. The match ended 1-1. On the other hand, the determination that every Irish player has in his armoury means we can take a little more interest than we normally would in the 'Boys in Green' in friendly internationals, especially as Trapattoni has to date fielded his best eleven regardless of the tie.

Paraguay travelled to Dublin for a World Cup warm-up at the RDS in May 2010. Us journalists received word in advance that the visitors had refused to train. Let's just say they wouldn't be putting their best foot forward. That made Ireland one of the bets of the century at 6/4. A victory ensued, confirming that the ear must be kept close to the ground or, failing that, the radio or television as kick-off approaches.

After tipping Italy and Spain, it was unlikely on the law of averages that I would have the winner of the 2010 World Cup up my sleeve. My intention was to repeat exactly my actions of 2006. Get involved heavily by laying at the Group Stage and then wind it down. I recommended on the radio that Mexico would beat South Africa in the opening game. I thought South Africa were a poor team and I was going against the argument that hosts positively exceed expectations. What I did personally was lay South Africa against Mexico at 2/1 and when the match finished in a draw, I was frustrated. The listeners would be rolling their eyes about losing money on my tip, whereas I had personally made a profit. I will campaign for laying to be in the lexicon.

France were on shaky ground in the same Group. Raymond Domenech, their coach, was unpopular and 'Les Bleus' were about to spectacularly implode. Nearly every Irish sports fan knew that France were no great shakes from the qualifying campaign and it seemed they were not mentally acclimatising to South Africa. I layed them against Uruguay at 11/8. A French players' revolt and an eventual surrender was underway, but on paper South Africa should never have beaten them in a million years. Bafana Bafana then did, at odds of 3/1. I didn't get involved and it was a regret. Sometimes you have to forget about paper and follow your own eyes. Then, at the start of the Euro 2012 qualifiers, a tidy Byelorussian team defeated France in Paris 1-0. Belarus went into that game at odds of 9/1. I received a call a couple of days later from Mr Crocodile. The football expert. He said he had been waiting five years for this result. Five years! He had backed Belarus to win and the draw to cover himself. It appeared by his tone that he had quite a bit on. He thundered the reasons down the phone. BATE Borisov in the Champions League – Alexander Hleb – a win over Holland. I listened intently. You always do when someone has backed a 9/1 winner. If it was me, I would have layed France, but he gained a much greater return from his knowledge being vindicated. He saw that France, in Laurent Blanc's first competitive game in charge, were still vulnerable. And Belarus were by no means a 9/1 shot. Post *Greece*, it seems that the margins between the great and the average in the international game are narrowing. Especially when the finalists of the 2006 World Cup, Italy and France, couldn't even qualify from the Group Stage four years later. It's something to note when examining the so-called 'lesser lights' in future qualifying campaigns and tournaments.

The 2010 World Cup was not as successful for me as 2006. The simple reason was that I too was busy in other parts of my life to be betting. And when you don't have a full focus on something, you should take time out. I was obviously going to get involved in some capacity, but my rolls of the dice were half-hearted. Unusually for me, I became involved in tipping in silly markets, like top goalscorer. I backed Brazil to win outright and Serbia to reach the quarter finals and neither team delivered. I was getting it wrong. I did lay with success, opposing Greece against South Korea, the USA against Ghana and Ghana against Uruguay. All of that money was eradicated when I backed England against Germany in the last 16 and Argentina against Germany in the last 8. They turned out to be two horrendous calls. I said "sod it" and backed Spain to win the trophy before the semi-finals at 9/4. So that recouped the Brazil and Serbia money, but I should have stuck to what I was good at, selective laying. As I couldn't do that as much as I would have liked in the Group Stage, it put me in a poor frame of mind to analyse the knockout stage, so no profit was made. Then again maybe I was just wrong. The problem is that when you are not a professional gambler, you can be idea-rich, but time-poor. When your head is not pointing you in the direction of profit, walk away from the particular sport until you come back with a cleansed mind.

# Chapter 13

## Gaelic Games

Ah yes, our national games. Senior hurling and senior football. The Gaelic Athletic Association. I enjoy betting on GAA matches and like other team sports, I keep it simple, backing counties for provincial or All-Ireland Senior Championship titles, or taking each fixture on a case by case basis. The inter-county championship runs from May until September in both codes (hurling and football) each year and that's where we will focus. Speaking in a personal rather than a professional capacity, I am indifferent to the National Leagues. They act as competitions in their own right, but serve as a warm-up for the respective championships. I'm a Clare hurling fan and it took sixty-three years for the Banner to win a Munster title from their victory in 1932 until their famous breakthrough in 1995. However, in the late 1970s, Clare were a very good team, winning leagues in 1977 and 1978. In those days the championships were based on a knockout structure and the Banner boys couldn't get out of Munster, losing the 1977 and 1978 provincial finals to Cork. And it was tough for the county to take, because the championship was, and is, *everything*. Nobody talks about Limerick's back-to-back hurling league wins in the 1980s, as all the nostalgia for the glory days is related to the All-Ireland win of 1973. Armagh won the 2005 football league title, but all I can recall is how they let it slip against Tyrone in the closing stages of that year's All-Ireland semi-final. Sure, it was nice for Laois to win the football league in 1986, but that doesn't even come close to the outpouring of emotion that greeted Mick O'Dwyer's warriors when they bridged a 57-year gap in Leinster in 2003. So I'm not going to advise on a betting strategy for the national leagues.

What is relevant is the impact the national leagues have on the senior championships in terms of form and whether you should bring that into your calculations for the summer. The evidence is very mixed. In football, Kerry have completed the league and championship double on three occasions in recent years, in 2004, 2006 and 2009. The 2010 All-Ireland winners Cork also won both competitions in the same year. In 2003, Tyrone landed the double. On the other hand, Donegal (2007) and Derry (2008) won the league and disappeared in each subsequent championship campaign. Mayo reached the 2010 league final and were humbled by Longford in the championship. My belief is that because there are two dominant counties in Munster football, it is easier for Kerry and Cork to have a good run at the league and not worry about suffering fatigue during the championship. Training for the elite inter-county teams is geared towards supreme physical and mental wellbeing in September – and nothing else. Tyrone were setting down a marker back in 2003 and that's why they came out of the blocks early on in the year. They would stay around for a while, as their collection of three Sam Maguire Cups would testify. And the performance of some counties in 2010 gives us food for thought when taking league form at face value. On the positive side, Down, who reached the All-Ireland final having started as 50/1 outsiders for the championship, performed well in the league and reached the Division 2 final. The league performance of Roscommon in Division 3 was poor, as they finished bottom of the table, but the Rossies then came out and won the Connacht title at odds of 8/1. Louth, who were cruelly denied a Leinster title by a refereeing blunder, were also a Division 3 team, while Limerick, who pushed eventual All-Ireland champions Cork to extra time in a qualifier, were a Division 4 outfit.

In hurling, Galway were very impressive throughout the league campaign, defeating Cork in the final, but the season could not have been viewed as a success after their one-point defeat to Tipperary in the All-Ireland quarter final. Kilkenny have taken the league seriously under the eye of manager Brian Cody. They won league and All-Ireland doubles in 2002, 2003, 2006 and 2009, but it was not a stretch for the Cats to dominate both competitions, due to their hegemony in the game over the last decade and a dwindling level of competition in the Leinster Championship prior to the arrival of Galway in 2009. Tipperary tend to take the league seriously when they have a good crop. They won the league and championship double in 2001 and won the league in 2008 in Liam Sheedy's first year in charge. They were beaten in extra time by Kilkenny in the 2009 final, and won the All-Ireland in 2010, so one can observe that they were building all the time. It is easier to do that in hurling, where the traditional powers (Kilkenny, Cork and Tipperary) have snuffed out any romantic breakthroughs since the turn of the millennium.

And that brings us on to our next point, which is how the championships have changed in the last fifteen years. In 1997, it was decided that counties in hurling would get a second chance, with the introduction of a 'back door' of qualifiers for defeated counties in the provinces. Beaten counties would face matches against other beaten counties and it would give them the chance to eventually qualify to face the winners of Munster and Leinster in the All-Ireland semi-finals. So Tipperary, who lost in the Munster final to Clare that year, beat defending champions Wexford to qualify for the All-Ireland final, which they lost (again) to Clare. Offaly became the first team to lose a provincial final and win an All-Ireland the following year. In football, the old system whereby the four provincial winners would be paired into semi-finalists, with the winners of those matches to meet in the final, was changed in 2001. Since then, we've seen much more exciting championships in hurling and football.

Although some flaws remain, Gaelic Games has grown as a sport over the past decade, an amateur sport that we can all be proud of. The change to the championship structures has resulted in a clear trend in both codes. The stronger counties have dominated the All-Ireland series. Since 1999, the traditional and most successful powers in *iománaíocht* – Kilkenny, Cork and Tipperary, have carved up the hurling championship between them, leaving Galway, Waterford, Clare, Limerick, Offaly and Wexford without invitations to the party. Between 2003 and 2009, Tyrone and Kerry shared the seven All-Irelands on offer in football and the 2010 winners Cork had reached six successive semi-finals before finally winning the Holy Grail. So when trying to unearth an outright winner before the championships, it's best to concentrate on the teams with a proven track record, or those, like Dublin's footballers in 2010, who may have started to knock on the door. Armagh's 2002 All-Ireland football win was a culmination of some decent years, which saw the Orchard County win Ulster and reach the last four in 1999 and 2000. Galway's hurlers are showing enough of late for one to think they could make the breakthrough, but Waterford, who have won four Munster crowns since 2002, have always discovered a county in their way in the pursuit of the Liam McCarthy Cup. It doesn't make the market terribly attractive for a punter, but that's the way it is, so it's best to stake more on a likely result than taking what looks to be a nice price on a county that may fall short. A 9/4 winner is better than a 20/1 loser.

And Cork were 9/4 shots to win the 2010 All-Ireland football championship, a tip I put up before the championship began in May. The reasons were clear. Cork were beaten finalists in 2007 and 2009 – only Kerry had beaten them in the championship since 2004 – and they had won the league with a bit in hand. It was a supermodel skinny price, too skinny when you consider they had to come through the qualifiers, beat Dublin with a very late knockout punch in the semi-final and then failed to fire until it became really urgent against Down in the final. In the end, Cork's class won through, but just about. Tipperary were also very short in the betting to win the All-Ireland hurling championship, at 5/2 back in May, especially as Kilkenny were going for five titles in a row. In fact, Tipp were a bigger price at 11/4 on the day of the All-Ireland final in September, which certainly opened my eyes to the value the bookies offer.

If you don't like betting on 9/4 shots over a six-month period, then the best area to snuff out value in GAA is through the provincial structure, or individual matches. And the only way you can do this is by closely watching the games and reading the tea-leaves ahead of each game. As mentioned, Roscommon won the 2010 Connacht football title at 8/1, partly because Galway and Mayo were in disarray – and Sligo had expended too much energy in beating the two traditional powers to reach the final. I took a position on Monaghan in

Ulster after they obliterated Fermanagh, but it was a naïve standpoint, as Tyrone made them look like schoolboys in the Ulster final. I was very strong on Meath against Dublin when they met in Leinster. Dublin had won five Leinster titles in a row, but such statistics can sometimes be used as gospel by the bookmakers, especially when there is a second chance for teams now. Meath were 9/5, which was an exceptional price, as they had reached the All-Ireland semi final in 2009 and Dublin were hopeless against Wexford in their first-round match. Meath put five goals past Dublin that day, but in the long run, Dublin coped with their defeat and discovered much better form in reaching the last four. Tipperary went down to Cork for the first round of the Munster hurling championship as red-hot favourites, but I felt they were still nursing a hangover from the 2009 All-Ireland final. I recommended the Rebels at 13/8, not because I believed Tipp were finished, but it was a simple opinion on a game on its own merits. Also, it took Tipperary from 1923 until 2008 to beat Cork at Páirc Uí Chaoimh, so that came into my mind. Home advantage matters. I have sided with the Rebels at home against Kerry in football. It appears to be the only venue where Cork don't turn into jelly against the Kingdom and they were a good bet to beat them in replays in Munster in 2006 (at 4/1) and in 2009 (at 6/4). I recommended both options, but Kerry have held the upper hand against their near neighbours at HQ. Cork were crushed at Croker in 2002, 2005, 2006, 2007, 2008 and 2009.

Now the key for us as punters is to correctly predict when Cork will break that Croke Park hoodoo against Kerry, because they will be a decent price when they do. Perhaps with an All-Ireland in the locker, it may happen for the Leesiders sooner rather than later. Meath were 15/2 to win the 2010 Leinster title, which was a good price for 2009 semi-finalists, but not as good as the 66/1 that was available on Louth to come out on top in the province for the first time in fifty-three years. It was all about the Kildare game for Louth – if they could win that – they were in with a squeak, as they were on the better side of the draw. They did, and were dreadfully unlucky not to beat Meath. It's not a cue to start looking for rank outsiders to make you rich. Fermanagh and Limerick have gone close but failed in recent years in Ulster and Munster, so it's best to remain in thrall to the bigger counties in the war for profit.

If you talk to fellow gamblers about GAA matches, a prediction of a draw is always somewhere in the conversation. If it's not, I often find I'm ringing a friend back to say – "What about the draw?" – and we both mumble to each other, agreeing in a self-satisfied manner, until we see Team A defeat Team B by ten points on the day. I have been tipping the draw in the All-Ireland hurling final for the last number of years, to the point where I have invited ridicule upon myself from the listeners. The simple fact is that there hasn't been a draw in a senior hurling final since 1959. Hurling is a game played at tremendous speed, which is why the odds of a draw can stretch to 16/1, more than double that of a 70-minute football market. I am going to continue to back the draw in the hurling final, because I am convinced on the law of averages that it will happen and a profit will accrue before we reach the twelfth try (the odds in 2010 were 12/1). I have been told that I am throwing money into a black hole, and that a draw may never happen in my lifetime, but isn't that the whole point of betting? Attempting to predict is the discipline. All you can do is look at the statistics, which say that 3 of the last 28 All-Ireland hurling semi-finals going back to the first year of the new format in 1997 have been draws. That's an average of just over 1 in 9. Also, 5 of the last 24 Munster deciders have finished in a stalemate first time out, an average of less than 1 in 5. An average of 0 for 51 in hurling finals is a complete anomaly, so I will keep investing in the draw on the first Sunday in September. I advise you to do the same. Hopefully it won't be another fifty-one years by the time it eventually occurs. I have visions of jumping up and down at Croke Park when the whistle confirms a draw in the hurling final. It's become a bit of an unhealthy obsession.

In 2010, you would have made a profit of €24 off a €1 stake if you had blindly backed the 70-minute draw in each of the 89 Championship matches in hurling and football between May and September. There were three draws in hurling (Offaly v Antrim 16/1, Galway v Offaly 16/1, and Waterford v Cork 11/1). There were eight draws in football (Kerry v Cork 15/2, Meath v Laois 8/1, Wexford v Dublin 14/1, Galway v Sligo 8/1,

Donegal v Down 7/1, Kildare v Antrim 8/1, Offaly v Clare 8/1 and Limerick v Cork 10/1). Now these were the best prices on offer, which means you must do your weekly shopping at various stores.

Draws are in the collective psyche when it comes to GAA, because the inter-county season is relatively short and there's the human element of having to spend money on tickets and travel to see your county again. However, draws don't occur as often as we would think. Since 2001, when the back door applied to football as well as hurling, the only other guaranteed year for profit with blind backing was 2007, when there were five draws in each code. Most of the time if you went in blind you would be looking at a significant loss. Just use common sense. Tyrone and Armagh have dominated the Ulster Championship in recent years, but it still remains very competitive throughout. Ulster matches can turn into physical, suffocating, low-scoring affairs, which increases the likelihood of a draw. I remember tipping Tyrone and Armagh to draw the provincial final in 2005. Kerry and Cork have played 19 times in the Championship since 2002 and drawn on 5 occasions, including in each of the last three seasons. So if you estimate that the price of a football draw is 7/1, you would have made a profit on Kerry and Cork in recent times, regardless of the losses. There are a lot less matches in hurling and scores are more frequent, so unless you share my religious fervour about the hurling final, I would limit draw betting to competitive football encounters. And the key to profit is to be selective when doing so. There are freak years such as 2007, when the Limerick v Tipperary hurling saga contributed to a season with five draws, but the year before that, there were no draws in the hurling championship. Now where did I put that jar of money for the draw in next year's hurling final . . . ?

# Chapter 14

## Rugby and Tennis

### Rugby

The small matter of the oval ball. I didn't exit the womb with a rugby ball in my hand, that's for sure. A sliotar, yes, a toy horse with a little fluffy mane, yes, a soccer ball without branding, yes. So while I love watching rugby and tuned into what was the Five Nations Championship as a boy, I never really understood the muddy club scene, with players wearing letters instead of numbers and kicking this awful brown contraption about in bitter January. Let's just say I wasn't a fan of *Rugby Special* on the BBC. However, when I have engaged in rugby tipping, it can be the most obvious sport, because it's down to form and there aren't many shocks.

Rugby is a much more 'ad-hoc' game than say, soccer when it comes to fixtures, so when we are looking at the big events, what are we considering? The Six Nations, obviously. The Heineken European Cup. The Tri

Nations. The World Cup. And maybe the Magners League. That's about it. So this will be short and sweet, because when it comes to rugby, I'm a firm believer that less is more. It's not down to knowledge, as simplicity is also the secret to successful Soccer and GAA betting. There are just more opportunities in those sports. And I'm not too much of a fan of long-term bets on a knockout competition such as the European Cup, where you may be a Leinster fan and you back them to win the European Cup in September and you are counting your money until they get done by a dodgy referee in the final minute of the semi-final in France the following April. At least the Premier League is based on a nine-month weekly process. And personally, I find it easier to size up the All-Ireland series in Gaelic games as a knockout competition. Immediacy is the better route when it comes to parting with cash in rugby. Six Nations immediacy over a period of about six weeks is the limit for me.

There are plenty of markets in rugby, that's for sure. And that's the problem. What I don't like about rugby betting is that the bookmakers seem to think that the result is pre-ordained before the start. Fair enough, Munster win 99 times out of 100 at Thomond Park, but the bookmakers make the handicap market as the basis for their marketing of betting on the sport. The handicap market is where each team is quoted at the same price and gets an artificial lead or starts the match in arrears. For example, Ireland were offered at 10/11 to beat Scotland with minus 14 points in the 2010 Six

Nations match at Croke Park. So Scotland were offered at 10/11 with a 14-point lead. They didn't need it because they won the match anyway at 6/1. I don't like handicap bets. In my mind, it's difficult to estimate how a match will proceed. For example, let's say hypothetically that Ireland play New Zealand. Ireland start brilliantly and go in at half time only 3 points behind. In the second half, New Zealand get on top and Ireland eventually run out of puff, conceding two late tries. So the handicap market may not reflect what really went on, as a team like Ireland may not be able to exert any more in the final few minutes. Alternatively, New Zealand could dominate the match and open up a 30-point lead before taking off their star names, allowing Ireland to score consolation tries, which would skew the handicap bet again. You could argue that such a sequence of events is possible in any sporting fixture, but rugby betting is based on the effing handicap. If I am looking for a simple match bet on rugby, I find I am navigating nonsense for ten minutes on an industry website.

One tip I was very proud of was putting up Ireland to win the Six Nations Grand Slam in 2009 at 9/1. This was based on Ireland's consistent performances over the previous decade, and the acknowledgement that perhaps Declan Kidney could bring the freshness required to take Ireland over the try line after Eddie O'Sullivan had fallen short. I said, "Why not?" on the airwaves, arguing the case that Wales had won two Grand Slams in 2005 and 2008 with an arguably inferior side. 9/1 was great, but I cannot see a 100/1 winner of the Six Nations in the future. Bizarrely, Scotland were available at that price of 100/1 before the start of the 1999 Five Nations Championship, which they won on points difference over England. Scotland had a poor season the year before, but they were coached by the respected Jim Telfer and made a mockery of such a price in a five-horse race.

I also tipped France for the 2010 Six Nations at 6/4, after watching the performances of their club sides in Europe and seeing that their coach, Marc Lièvremont, was getting serious with eighteen months to go to the World Cup. Ireland were always a major lay for the 2010 season after the year-long euphoria that followed the incredible win over Wales in Cardiff. The country's last Grand Slam was in 1948. Ireland entered 2010 at just 5/1 to win the Grand Slam again with trips to France and England on the horizon. What were people expecting? World Domination! That was a monster lay. I saw the 2009 campaign as a culmination after years of close calls for Ireland, rather than a beginning. It's not hard to identify the patterns in rugby, which is why I discount the complicated markets on matches and just look at placing the occasional bigger bet on individual occurrences.

And Ireland's Six Nations price in 2010 brings me to that auld chestnut again, patriotism. I've touched on it before and I think it applies more to Irish rugby than the Republic of Ireland soccer team, who haven't beaten a decent football nation away from home in a qualifier since 1987. Every year I go to Cheltenham and I see Irish punters lumping money on Irish horses just because they are Irish. I will never forget the first day of the 2002 Festival, when Like A Butterfly and Moscow Flyer won the first two races for Ireland, and the crowd then just steamed in to back Ireland's Istabraq for the Champion Hurdle at 2/1. Rose-tinted cash. If you had been listening to TODAY FM the previous week, you would have known that we reported (after a top source told me) that Istabraq had leg trouble and was a doubt for the Champion Hurdle. Trainer Aidan O'Brien denied our report in a front-page story in the *Racing Post* the following day. What happened in the race? Istabraq was pulled up by jockey Charlie Swan after just two hurdles with a tendon injury. The point is not that people were backing the 10-year-old Istabraq because they felt he was the most likely winner, they waded in as part of the Irish tide after the first two races. I spoke to a number of people afterwards who confirmed this view. I've mentioned the English soccer team before – and I'm always flabbergasted by the amount of partisan money that is placed by supporters when Liverpool play Manchester United, or when Munster take to the field. If you are guilty at this, stop. Never back your own team or country just because it's your team. You belong enough by going to the matches, spending money on replica shirts, defending them in the pub and corrupting your children by ensuring they follow your lead. Unless it's incredibly enjoyable to your being, you don't need to bet on them. Only bet on them if you have a genuine dispassionate belief that they can win. So, with Ireland in rugby, there's no point in us backing them due to national pride. I would much rather back England at the Aviva Stadium if I thought they were going to beat Ireland and were a decent price to do so.

England were 7/4 to win the 2003 World Cup, and that was another tip I put up, based once again on form. They had won the Grand Slam in Dublin earlier that year and then followed that up with wins over New Zealand and Australia in the Southern Hemisphere. They were the number-one-ranked team in the world and an absolute banker as far as I was concerned. So, I admit, I was clapping when Jonny Wilkinson kicked that drop goal.

1991 aside, and that was really only for one game in our own backyard against Australia, Ireland have generally underperformed at the World Cup. We usually meet France at some stage and then it's all over. Nobody could have predicted the extent of the 2007 debacle to make money on it, but from a betting perspective, until Ireland display serious intent before a World Cup, I wouldn't touch them.

As with first-goalscorer market in soccer, I also don't like first-tryscorer odds. Predicting who is at the bottom of a rolling maul at the whitewash is hard enough for the commentators without trying to be a genie yourself and guess who will be the first player out of 30 to ground the ball. There is a top tryscorer market for the entire Six Nations, which has produced some odd results in recent years. If you are going to get involved in it, it's best to have an idea of which country will win the Championship. In 2009, Ireland won the Grand Slam and Brian O'Driscoll was the joint top try scorer at 33/1. In 2008, Wales swept all before them and Shane Williams took the honours at 16/1. Ireland came up just short in 2007, but Ronan O'Gara was the joint top tryscorer at an incredible 125/1. Four players, Tommy Bowe at 8/1, Williams at 14/1, Keith Earls at 40/1 and Jamie Hook at 66/1 shared the prize in 2010. What I noticed was that Earls went into Munster's subsequent Heineken Cup semi-final against Biarritz at 16/1 to be the first tryscorer, which was surprising, given a) he was in form, and b) he is an attacking back. I suppose I shouldn't scoff at a price of 33/1 about O'Driscoll. BOD is always a dangerous man in any tournament and he is a centre.

Isn't a draw such a damp squib in rugby? Whenever I have watched a rugby game end in a draw, I am looking around to ask "What now?". Ireland have not drawn a game in the Six Nations since 1994, when it was still the Five Nations. There have only been 3 draws in the Six Nations in the last decade and if you consider there are 15 Six Nations games in a campaign, that's an average of 1 in 50, significantly more than a bookmaker would offer. Changing the number of points for a try from 4 to 5 didn't help draw backers, so it's a bet I would avoid, both in the match market and the handicap market. Anyway, I have missed the ferry on the 80-minute draw. I was considering it before the 2003 World Cup Final between England and Australia and I didn't do it. It paid 18/1.

In terms of the European Cup from an overall perspective – given their history of heartbreaks, it was very difficult to select Munster to win the Heineken Cup until they actually got over the line, which they finally managed to do in 2006. It would have been easier to predict their 2008 success, although the odds by that stage were prohibitive. I always wanted to find the team to catch Munster in the European Cup at Thomond Park, since their unbeaten record there had begun to take on otherworldly status. Luckily I spotted that Leicester, the team which defeated Munster in the 2002 Final (know your history) had only gone down narrowly in the Pool Stage of the 2006-7 competition at Welford Road. I had a sneaking suspicion that their pack would trouble Munster and I put them up in January 2007 at 13/8. Leicester won, breaking that unbelievable record. As would be the case with Ireland in 2009, I was trying to get a sense for something before it actually happened. It's a constant refrain in this book. And that's why I was kicking myself when I decided not to do the double of Toulouse and Biarritz to beat the Irish provinces in the 2010 semi-finals at 15/8. These matches came after an intense two years for the Irish players, some of whom had donned the green of Ireland and the red of the Lions. Munster had shown some deficiencies against Perpignan and Northampton Saints that had worried me. Leinster crawled over the line against Clermont Auvergne in their quarter final. Some bookmakers had made Munster and Leinster invincible, but winning in France is not easy, as we have seen down through the years. So I was really annoyed that I didn't follow up on the courage of my convictions and do the bet. I was so frustrated that I felt like going into Elverys, buying a rugby ball, and bursting it.

## Tennis

There were tears in my eyes on the day Goran Ivanisevic won Wimbledon in 2001. He was my favourite tennis player after the departures of Boris Becker and Martina Navratilova. Sport can be cruel and a fairytale like Goran's isn't always written. That men's singles final between the Croat and Pat Rafter had it all: five sets; a Monday finish in front of a boisterous crowd; and the right conclusion as Ivanisevic finally got his paws on the gold trophy (9-7 in the fifth) after losing three finals. I loved watching Goran play because he wore his heart on his sleeve on court. He was a brilliant big server of the ball, unleashing ace after ace, which was totally suited to what was then a new era of grass-court tennis. And I, as a fan, was thrilled for the guy after he lost a final he should have won to Andre Agassi in 1992, and then fell to the dominant Pete Sampras in 1994 and 1998.

In 2000, I backed Ivanisevic to win Wimbledon at large odds. I can't remember what price he was, but he was ranked 65th in the world at the time, so it was more of a sentimental wager. It was thus personally bittersweet when he won twelve months later as a wildcard, ranked 125th in the world, at odds of 150/1.

I knew then and I know now that I will never back a tennis winner at that price. Maybe that's why I divorced tennis betting and shacked up in a fleabag motel with golfers and the odd filly, because like most sports-mad kids, I watched a lot of tennis growing up. Wimbledon was a big part of my summer, and late June and early July meant taking a racquet to the park to imitate Jimmy Connors. I was good at the yelling on the serve, but little else.

The reality is that Roger Federer and Rafael Nadal have made tennis a much less attractive sport to find betting angles on in recent years. I find the women's game a little bizarre – the Williams sisters dominate when they are fit and focused – the Belgians come out of retirement and win – and then you have the crazy 100/1 shocks like Francesca Schiavone in the 2010 French Open. What all of this says to me is that the women's game has been lacking in depth, when you consider past giants such as Navratilova, Chris Evert, Steffi Graf and Monica Seles.

Perhaps because of this unpredictability, I have never tipped a ladies singles outcome on the radio. In 2003, I gave a hat trick of winners in the men's Grand Slams – Juan Carlos Ferrero at 11/4 in the French Open, Federer at 5/1 at Wimbledon, and Andy Roddick at 11/4 in the US Open. Since then, of the 28 men's Grand Slam titles on offer, Federer and Nadal have won 24 of them. It's pretty depressing, isn't it? When you go from Ivanisevic at 150/1 to Nadal in Paris at 8/13 or Federer in Melbourne at 1/2, you have to wonder – what is the point? I followed David Nalbandian for a while, but he failed to deliver – and although I believe Andy Murray will win a Grand Slam, at the time of writing he has yet to make the breakthrough. We will have to wait for the Federer and Nadal era to wane before the tasty prices return. What I have learned from observing tennis betting down through the years is that the saying – 'form is temporary, class is permanent' is very true. I don't know who coined that saying, but it is the case in every one of the four Grand Slams as I will illustrate. And we will only look at the Grand Slams. Let's not complicate it. The regular tour isn't popular enough.

Your starting point for the four Grand Slams is the surfaces on which they are played. The Australian and US Opens are held on hard courts (a form of concrete); the French Open is played on clay; and Wimbledon, as we all know, is for lovers of grass. You can often draw a line through certain players on certain surfaces – and that is always an advantage if you are a layer in the market – no matter how good a respective player's form is ahead of a tournament. For example, despite their dominance on the court and in the public eye, John McEnroe, Pete Sampras and Boris Becker never won the French Open. They loved to serve and volley and the slower surfaces of Roland Garros found them out. Ivan Lendl, who was a specialist in Paris, never won Wimbledon, and Bjorn Borg, who was a specialist everywhere else, failed on the hard courts of Flushing Meadows. In the ladies' game, Monica Seles was brilliant on clay, but less effective on grass. Justine Henin and

Kim Clijsters have not been able to close the deal at Wimbledon, while power-hitters Venus Williams and Maria Sharapova have struggled in Paris. It is sink or swim on the surface for many players, which is not surprising when the skills are specific and the margins at the top are as thin as a McEnroe-challenged baseline call.

Of course, recent form is a major factor in placing any bet, but remember that we've been living through an era in tennis where there is cream at the top and the rest is old milk. Federer has won 16 Grand Slam singles titles since 2003. Nadal has landed 9 Grand Slam singles titles since 2005 and the Williams sisters have won 20 Grand Slam singles titles between them. So you cannot discount talent when scouring the field. For these players, it's all about winning the four big tournaments. So when Serena Williams, ranked 81st in the World, after undergoing knee surgery and personal trauma in the wake of the death of her half-sister, crushed Maria Sharapova 6-1, 6-2 in the 2007 **Australian Open** ladies' singles final, it was a surprise. A surprise, but it shouldn't have been a shock. Serena Williams had won the Australian Open twice before, in 2003 and 2005, so she knew what to do. In fact, she made a mockery of her odds of 20/1. The same goes for Roger Federer, who was 11/4 to win the 2010 Australian Open! Perhaps his generous price was a result of losing the previous year's decider to Nadal and the 2009 US Open final to Juan Martin Del Potro, but Federer was a three-time winner in Melbourne and his price underestimated his chance.

It's important to examine form on hard courts before you make your picks in Australia. Marat Safin and Maria Sharapova won US Open titles in advance of triumphing in Melbourne – while Novak Djokovic has always excelled on asphalt, so his win at odds of 8/1 in 2008 after reaching the previous season's US Open Final could have been predicted. The issue of late has been in attempting to tell when Federer and Nadal are not going to fire, which is not often.

Federer was a 6/1 shot to take the 2009 **French Open** title. He never looked like bettering Nadal in their previous meetings in Paris, but Nadal, although close to it at times, is not superhuman. His incredible unbeaten record going back to 2005 was always going to end at some stage. Robin Soderling was the villain in the 2009 semi-final. So while you couldn't lay Nadal, Federer was a nice price in what was effectively a two-man race. Andre Agassi was also an exceptional price at 33/1 in 1999, given he had three Grand Slam titles in the locker and had lost the final in Paris in 1990 and 1991. The likes of Thomas Muster, Sergi Bruguera, Gustavo Kuerten and Carlos Moya had almost ring-fenced clay-court tennis in the 90s, performing well in the warm-up events, taking that to Paris, and not letting the rest have a shot. However, Agassi was still on the world radar, at number 14 when he won, which is why you need to have a long memory. My selection for Ferrero back in 2003 was obvious. He had lost the previous year's final and had won a good tournament in Monte Carlo earlier that year. The same rationale was used for tipping

Guillermo Coria a year later. The Argentine was the king of clay at that time and looked set to win in Paris until he wobbled at two sets to love up against Gaston Gaudio, a 66/1 chance, in the final. And then along came Nadal.

As for the ladies at the French – because the Williams sisters have not been strong in Paris (one win for Serena in 2003) – Justine Henin has dominated, with four titles in five years between 2003 and 2007. Henin is deadly from the baseline and possesses a terrifying backhand which is suited to Roland Garros. Ana Ivanovic (in 2008 at 15/2) and Svetlana Kuznetsova (in 2009 at 7/1) were beaten finalists in previous years, so you could have made an argument for them, but Iva Majoli in 1997, Anastasia Myskina in 2004 (50/1) and Francesca Schiavone in 2010 were rank outsiders. Therefore it's best to keep an open mind with the fairer sex in gay Paris.

I could see Federer coming at **Wimbledon** in 2003, and I could see his fall in 2010. Whether his defeat by Tomas Berdych in 2010 was the beginning of the end, I don't know, but his loss to Lleyton Hewitt in a warm-up event in Halle rang alarm bells in my head and I confidently pressed the lay button on Federer in advance of Wimbledon at 6/4. I remember advising people to lay him on Twitter, but unfortunately the outright winner wasn't as clear for me, so I erred in tipping Andy Murray and not Nadal at 5/2. In hindsight, I should have remembered that 'class is permanent', but I was a little bit worried about Nadal's fitness going into the All England Club, musings which were completely misguided. That's why I prefer to lay at times and leave it at that. In 2003, Federer was a fantastic bet at 5/1, as he had ended the Sampras era on grass in 2001 and was ready to step up and become a true great. Unfortunately, that's the last time he was a price worth taking in London. What I will be looking closely at is whether Federer has another big push in him. He's only approaching 30, but after so long at the summit the window is closing all the time, especially with Nadal, the undisputed new world number one – ascendant on all surfaces.

The 'class is permanent' argument has applied to Venus Williams at Wimbledon. She's lifted that gold plate five times and it's her best surface. She came from the clouds to win at 20/1 in 2005, but as a dual winner in 2000 and 2001 – ranked number 14 – and approaching the Championship at only the age of 25, she was great value in the betting to prevail, as she did in the final against Lindsay Davenport. So I cannot understand, on reflection, why she was 16/1 to win again in 2007 on the back of a quiet build-up. Nobody had analysed 2005, it seems. I certainly didn't. A seeding of 23 and a world ranking of 31 for Venus didn't matter a hoot in 2007. Have I annoyed you with the 'class is permanent' mantra yet? We know the lessons going forward. Check the surfaces. Look for repeat winners. Who was the top lady at Wimbledon in 2009 and 2010? Serena Williams. Unlike Martina Hingis, the Californians have shown tremendous durability throughout their careers.

Another lady with more strings to her racquet was Kim Clijsters, who, after a spell of over two years in retirement, won the 2009 **US Open** at odds of 16/1. Now you couldn't have thrown a score on her with any confidence. It was only her third tournament back, but she'd obviously been working hard, was fit and with a weak field she shocked everyone. Clijsters did a 'Williams' on it, so to speak – she had won the US Open back in 2005 at a much skinnier price of 9/4. Clijsters came back to successfully defend her US Open crown in 2010 as the number 2 seed. And in general, the US Open tends to go to the form player in both the men's and ladies' singles. Venus Williams won Wimbledon and the US Open in 2000 and 2001; Henin's victories in 2003 and 2007 were not unexpected (she had taken the French in 2003 and was the number 2 seed in the draw and four years later she was the top-ranked player in the world). Maria Sharapova was the third seed when she won in 2006, while Serena Williams added to her Wimbledon crowns in 2002 and 2008 by tasting further glory in New York. The only shock was Svetlana Kuznetsova, a 33/1 outsider in 2004, but she was only 19. Remember that all good careers start somewhere. All great champions break through. Maybe she was inspired by fellow Russian Sharapova, a stunning winner at Wimbledon at the age of 17 that year.

On the men's side, Pete Sampras struck a blow for the 'class is permanent' brigade with a career capping 28/1 victory in 2002. By that stage, Sampras was washed up in many people's eyes as an elite tennis player. He was a beaten docket. However, this was Pete Sampras, the man who won the US Open at the age of

19 in 1990. A thirteen-time Grand Slam winner entering the fray at Flushing Meadows. Respect a legend. To change sports for thirty seconds as an example: 52-year-old Steve Davis beat John Higgins in the 2010 World Snooker Championship. Anyway, Sampras silenced the doubters by winning his fifth US Open. Federer won five successive US Opens from 2004 to 2008. His price got steadily worse before each year, to the point that when he lined up before the 2007 renewal, he was 8/15.

Recent form played a big part in the victories of Andy Roddick in 2003, Juan Martin Del Potro (at 14/1) in 2009 and Nadal in 2010. Roddick had reached the last four of the Australian Open and won a hard-court tournament before his success; Del Potro took four successive tournaments in 2008 and tested Federer in the 2009 French semi-final before shocking the Swiss a few months later; and Nadal, the champion that he is, became only the seventh man to win a career Grand Slam in 2010. He'll be attempting to simultaneously hold all four Grand Slam trophies in Australia in 2011, and when you read this line of the book, you'll already know the result.

# Epilogue

## *It's Your Money and You'll Win if You Want to*

I place two mobile phones on a table. I am the only person in the room.

I type a number into Phone A and ring it. Phone B rings on the table. I pick up phone A and I say in an officious manner, "Is that Mr Duggan?"

I pick up Phone B and reply, "Yes."

Phone A: "Mr Duggan, this is your accountant. In relation to that loan you requested . . ."

Phone B: Silence . . . "Yes."

Phone A: "I am pleased to say that the bank will be able to meet your request."

Phone B: "Great. Thank you."

Phone A: "€1,000 over two years, wasn't it?"

Phone B: "Yes, it was."

Phone A: "What was it for again, remind me? They want to know."

Phone B: "Oh, I just wanted some money for the odd

extra-curricular activity that doesn't fall under day-to-day expenditure – you know, a bit of golf, some football games, maybe to go to the races from time to time."

Phone A: "Oh, of course. Sorry for being so remiss. Well, the repayment terms are €50 a month into the loan account. So that's a total repayment of €1,200 over the 24 months. I'll send out the documents to your house. Have a good day, Mr Duggan."

Phone B: "Thank you."

If you want to properly engage in sports betting, this is a good way to start. You have given yourself a loan. This loan is not a short-term cash-injection for a holiday, but should be looked upon as a capital investment. I find that holding a certain amount of capital is important when it comes to betting – if you have funds to play with, it allows you to build profit at a steady rate. It's a better solution than depositing €20 into an online account repeatedly, trying to win money too quickly and becoming annoyed when you lose. It's better to start with more money and a long-term approach. It will help you to remain mentally content and sharp. The onus is on you to pay back the lender (you) €50 a month. Now you don't want this to be a household expense, so that will guarantee you spend your €1,000 wisely. You also don't want to blow it in four months and realise you still owe the principal for the next two years. After all, it is *your* money.

# Glossary of Terms

**Accumulator:**

A cumulative multiple bet in which the punter makes a number of selections and the winnings from the first selection carry onto the next one and so on. All selections must win for the bet to be a success.

**A distance:**

A winning margin in horse-racing of over 30 lengths.

**All-weather:**

An artificial surface on which racing is held all year round. Ireland's all-weather track is Dundalk.

**Ante-post:**

Prices put up by the bookmakers in advance of the day of the event. In horse-racing, better odds may be offered, but the stake is lost if the horse doesn't run.

**Apprentice:**

An inexperienced jockey who receives a weight concession for racing against more experienced rivals.

**Away form:**

The performance of a team away from home. Important for soccer analysis.

**Backing:**

Betting on an outcome to occur.

**Backing blind:**

Backing a team or an individual every time they participate until they win.

***Bad Lieutenant*:**

A 1992 film about a corrupt New York homicide detective, played by Harvey Keitel.

**Ball striking:**

What a golfer does from the tee and the fairway before the putter is taken out of the bag.

**Banker:**

A selection which is very strongly fancied, which is often included in combination bets.

Birdie:

A score of 1 under par on a golf hole.

*Blade Runner*:

A 1982 science-fiction movie. Directed by Ridley Scott and set in a dystopian future.

Board:

A traditional bookmaker's infrastructure for showing prices.

Bogey:

1 over par on a golf hole.

Bookmaker:

The individual or entity you must defeat.

Bottle:

In this instance, what a golfer must possess to win a tournament.

Bottomless:

Very heavy ground in racing.

Bumper:

A flat race for National Hunt horses, usually over 2 miles.

Canadian:

A multiple of 26 bets (10 doubles, 10 trebles, 5 four-fold accumulators and 1 five-fold accumulator) with selections in 5 different events. It's also called a Super Yankee.

Claret Jug:

What they present to the winner of golf's Open Championship.

Clay:

In tennis, the surface on which they play the French Open.

Clutch putter:

A golfer who doesn't miss under pressure from short distances (i.e. 6 feet). It's usually to save par.

Co-Favourites:

When there are three or more competitors at the same price at the top of the market.

*Columbo*:

An American TV detective series set in Los Angeles, starring Peter Falk as the lead character, the dishevelled but wily Lieutenant Columbo.

Course:

> Where a race is run, or a golf tournament is played. Very important for golf form study.

Cut:

> The point midway through a golf tournament when the field is reduced to half, based on score.

D'Arby, Terence Trent:

> A 1980s American pop singer, who penned a hit entitled 'If You Let Me Stay'.

Dead heat:

> When two horses cannot be separated by the photo. If you back a horse to win and the race finishes in a dead heat, the win part of the bet is settled to half your stake. If you back a golfer each way and the terms are the first five places, if he finishes in a three-way tie for fourth, you lose a third of your stake.

Declarations:

> When horses are confirmed as entrants for racing 24 or 48 hours in advance.

Doing your brains:

> Losing all your money, usually after losing control of your discipline.

Double:

One bet on two selections in different events. Both selections must win for the Double to pay.

Double bogey:

2 over par on a golf hole.

Double carpet:

Slang for the winning price we all love, 33/1.

Draw bias:

In flat racing, the starting stalls may be near a bend, allowing some horses to take the shortest route around the bend. This bias gives horses drawn either low or high in the stalls an advantage. Ground conditions may also determine if it is better for a horse to be drawn low or high, as there may be quicker ground at one end of the track.

Draw no bet:

When a bookmaker (often in soccer) removes the draw from the market. A draw will result in your stake being refunded.

Drifter:

A competitor which is friendless in the betting market and lengthens in price.

Dual forecast:

Picking two horses to finish first and second in either order.

Each way:

A win bet and a place bet together.

Eagle:

2 under par on a golf hole.

Exchange:

A betting market where the punters set the odds and back and lay against one another.

Fold:

Combines with a number, signifying the number of selections in a multiple bet. (e.g. four-fold)

Forecast:

In racing, selecting two horses to finish first and second in the correct order. On the Tote, it is known as the Exacta.

Furlong:

A distance of one eighth of a mile, or 220 yards, or 201 metres.

Goldilocks Optimum:

A term used to describe the US economy of the mid- and late-1990s as "not too hot, not too cold, but just right" like Goldilocks' porridge.

Goliath:

The life-changing bet. A multiple consisting of 247 bets (28 doubles, 56 trebles, 70 four-fold accumulators, 56 five-folds, 28 six-folds, 8 seven-folds and 1 eight-fold) involving 8 selections in different events. 2 of your selections must win to guarantee a return.

Good:

On the race track, it means a decent surface for racing without much water underfoot.

Good to firm:

Faster than good.

Good to soft:

Good ground with some rain in it, making the surface a little more testing for horses.

Grand:

A thousand euro/pounds.

Grass:

In tennis, the surface on which they play Wimbledon.

Green:

An inexperienced horse or a putting surface for golfers. Or the colour of this book.

Group/Graded Race:

The top races in flat/National Hunt off level weights.

Guineas:

Old coin used in the United Kingdom up to two centuries ago. Its value was eventually fixed at 21 shillings. A guinea would equate to £1.05 today.

Handicap:

In racing, this is where horses carry different weights in a race in order to give every horse the same chance on form. In other sports, a team may receive a points bonus or deficit in a handicap market to even the sides up.

Hard Court:

In tennis, the surface on which they play the Australian Open and US Open.

Heavy:

Ground which has taken a lot of rain, giving an advantage to stamina-laden horses.

Heinz:

There are 57 varieties. It's a multiple bet consisting of 57 bets (15 doubles, 20 trebles, 15 four-fold accumulators, 6 five-fold accumulators and 1 six-fold accumulator) involving 6 selections in different events.

Hindenburg:

A German airship which caught fire and was destroyed in New Jersey in 1937, shattering public confidence in the airship as a method of transport.

Home form:

The performance of a team in their own backyard. Important for soccer analysis.

*Iománaíocht*:

The word '*As Gaeilge*' for hurling.

Jackpot:

In racing, a Tote bet on course where you need to select the winners of races 3-6 in Ireland and the first 6 races in the UK. You can select more than one horse in each race and increase your outlay with combinations. The dividend is determined by the Tote taking a deduction and then dividing the pool by the number of winners.

Joint favourites:

When two competitors are the same price at the head of a market.

Jolly:

Slang for a favourite.

Juvenile:

In flat racing, a 2-year-old equine. In jumps racing, it refers to a 4-year-old hurdler.

Laying:

Taking bets on an outcome not to occur.

Laying off:

Reducing your profit or liabilities by opposing your earlier back or lay. Also known as hedging.

Links:

Golf courses on land adjoining the sea.

Long shot:

A selection at big odds that the bookmaker believes is unlikely to win.

Losing It:

Quoted at 100/1 on the front cover, it's what you cannot possibly do if you adhere to my fundamentals.

Lucky 15:

A Yankee with four singles.

Lucky 31:

A Canadian with five singles.

Lucky 63:

A Heinz with six singles.

Maiden:

A competitor which has yet to win an event.

Majors:

In golf, the four annual tournaments which bestow greatness.

Market:

Where betting happens, as people back against

the odds set by the bookmakers or other punters in the case of an exchange.

Money Back Special:

A friendly marketing device used by bookmakers to coax punters into a particular market.

Monkey:

Betting slang for 500 euro/pounds. I placed a monkey on Steve Flesch and won 50 monkeys.

Mister Ed:

The eponymous talking horse from a 1960s American sitcom.

Mr Crocodile:

A personal pseudonym for a friend of mine who is a soccer expert.

Nag:

Slang for a horse. I won't give the other definition.

Odds:

The price set by a bookmaker to reflect the probability in their opinion of an outcome occurring.

**Odds-against:**

A price greater than even money.

**Odds compiler:**

An expert employed by a bookmaker to set the odds and form a market.

**Odds-on:**

A price less than even money.

**Off:**

When a race begins. In terms of an inside gamble, when a horse is 'off', it is ready to win.

**Off the bridle:**

A horse that is under pressure from the jockey.

**On the bridle:**

A horse not under pressure from the jockey.

**On the nose:**

A bet on a competitor to win only.

**Outsider:**

See Long shot. A rank outsider is approaching 'rag' territory.

Over-round:

The percentage that determines the bookmaker's profit margin.

Pacemaker:

In horse-racing, it refers to a horse that runs very quickly from the front early on to ensure a true pace for a more fancied stablemate.

Par:

The predetermined amount of shots in professional golf in which a scratch player should complete a hole. If a golfer makes 3 birdies and no bogeys in a round of 18 holes, he is 3 under par for the day.

Patent:

A multiple bet consisting of 7 bets (3 singles, 3 doubles and 1 treble) on 3 different selections.

*PGA Tour Website*:

This is where you should spend a lot of your time going forward.

Photo finish:

In horse-racing, it's where the stewards are required to examine the photo at the finishing line to determine the winner between two or more horses.

Pink Euro notes:

€500. Other people may describe them as a shade of purple.

Place:

A bet on a selection to finish in the first three, four, five, six, seven or eight, dependent on the terms offered by the bookmaker.

Placepot:

A Tote bet in which the punter must successfully select a horse to be placed in successive races (usually the first six races). Constructed in a similar fashion to the Jackpot.

PlayStation:

A hugely popular computer console, which has some excellent golf games.

Pool:

Where everybody's bets are placed in a Tote system.

Pony:

Betting slang for 25 euro/pounds.

Price, Vincent:

An acclaimed American 20th Century actor, noted for his work in horror movies.

Punter:

The person who is trying to make money by betting on events. It's a nicer word than gambler.

Quadpot:

A placepot-style bet for four races on the card, rather than the usual six. It often attracts a bigger punter.

Rag:

A complete outsider that is there to make up the numbers. James Buster Douglas was a 42/1 rag against Mike Tyson in Tokyo.

*Racing Post*:

Horse-racing's industry newspaper. There is now an Irish version.

Recent form:

A very important consideration for any selection on any sport, but especially for golf.

Renewal:

In horse-racing, it is used to describe an on-going event which regularly recommences, i.e. the 2005 *renewal* of the Grand National.

Rookie:

Specifically related to golf, it means a player competing in a tournament for the first time or on tour for the first time.

Rule 4:

A deduction applied by bookmakers to dividends when a horse is withdrawn and there is not time for a new market to form.

Score:

Slang for 20 euro/pounds.

Seed:

A ranking of all players or teams in a tournament, so that the player or team which has the best previous record or form is drawn against weaker players/teams first. Seedings are framed so that the best players/teams should theoretically meet in the final.

Short odds:

When a competitor is at a low price in an

event. It usually reflects favouritism – i.e. Tiger Woods at 9/4 in a field of 100 golfers.

Single:

In betting, it's a bet on one individual outcome.

Skinner:

A winner that nobody has backed. Think 2003 Open winner Ben Curtis.

Soft:

Ground which has seen a lot of rain, increasing the demands of a horse's stamina to get through it.

Smoke the ball:

When a golfer drives the ball a long way from the tee, usually in an accurate manner.

Starting price:

The price of each horse at the beginning of the race. Otherwise known as the 'SP'.

Stake:

The amount of money placed on an outcome.

**Stewards:**

The gentlemen who watch racing to ensure the rules are being upheld.

**Sudden death:**

In golf, it refers to a play-off where extra holes are played to determine the winner of the tournament when the scores are tied. In soccer, it refers to a penalty shoot-out, when extra kicks are taken to determine the winner when the scores are tied in the shoot-out.

**Super Heinz:**

A multiple consisting of 120 bets (21 doubles, 35 trebles, 35 four-fold accumulators, 21 five-folds, 7 six-folds and 1 seven-fold) involving 7 selections in different events. 2 of your selections must win to guarantee a return.

**Taking a price:**

Stating that you would like to avail of the price currently offered by the bookmaker in anticipation of it shortening in the market.

**Team sheets:**

The line-ups for an event. In soccer, team sheets are not usually released until an hour before kick-off.

Tissue:

The prices or odds on each competitor in an event to predict its respective chance. Bookmakers may use odds compilers to form a tissue, but on an exchange, it is established by punters backing and laying against each other.

Ton:

Slang for 100 euro/pounds.

Tote:

An on-course totalisator run by horse-racing authorities which, as a form of sweepstake, pools people's bets and divides the winnings after taking a percentage.

Tote returns:

The dividend paid to winning units on the Tote at the racecourse following each race.

Touch:

An insider gamble on a horse.

Track:

Another term for racecourse.

**Treble:**

One bet on three different selections. All three selections must win for the bet to win.

**Trifecta:**

A Tote bet in which the first three horses must be selected in the correct order.

**Trixie:**

A patent without singles consisting of 4 bets (3 doubles and a treble) with selections on 3 different events.

**Turf Accountant:**

Another name for a licensed bookmaker.

**Weighed-in:**

What is declared at Cheltenham and other UK racetracks when the winning jockey's weight is confirmed as correct, allowing bets to be officially paid.

**Went off at:**

The starting price of the selection.

**Winner Alright:**

An Irish version of 'weighed-in'.

With the field:

Often used in exacta bets where you think you have found the winner and combine it with the remaining horses to generate a potentially decent dividend.

Yankee:

A multiple of 11 bets (6 doubles, 4 trebles, 1 four-fold accumulator) with selections in 4 different events.

Yielding:

An Irish description for going which is between good and soft.